THE BATTLEFIELD DIARIES

A JOURNEY THROUGH INDIA'S HEROIC PAST

RISHI RAJ

An imprint of
Srishti Publishers & Distributors

Srishti Publishers & Distributors
A unit of AJR Publishing LLP
212A, Peacock Lane
Shahpur Jat, New Delhi – 110 049

editorial@srishtipublishers.com

First Published in English by Bold,
an imprint of Srishti Publishers & Distributors in 2025

Originally published in Hindi by Prabhat Paperbacks in 2022

10 9 8 7 6 5 4 3 2 1

This is a work of non-fiction based on the author's research about the subject and interviews with their next of kin, friends and associates. While due care has been taken by the author and publisher to verify contents at press time, any inadvertent miss that is brought to their notice shall be duly verified and updated subsequently. Actual names of people and places have been used with a view to provide firsthand information.

Printed and bound in India.

Dedicated to
Shaheed-e-Azam
Bhagat Singh

FOREWORD

The 5th of July, 1999, is a date etched in my mind for eternity. I feel grateful to God that He selected me for this noble mission that I, along with my comrades, undertook. There was a fierce war going on with Pakistan. Tiger Hill, situated in Drass, Ladakh, a symbol of our self-respect and pride, was still under the disgraceful occupation of Pakistan. After fighting the enemy on the Tololing Peak for twenty-two days and unfurling the Tricolour there, I proceeded with my comrades to capture what was rightfully ours – Tiger Hill. As a disciplined soldier of the Indian Army, I desperately wanted to capture Tiger Hill with every fibre of my being. The time had come for me to prove my passion, valour and gallantry.

It was bone-chillingly cold at an altitude of 16,500 feet, and it was a steep climb to the top, to say the least. Six out of my seven comrades had made the supreme sacrifice as we fought with all our might. Hit by three bullets, I was badly wounded. But that did not diminish my fervour in any way, nor did I feel any pain. I attacked the Pakistani soldiers with a grenade and killed four of them. I don't know where the power to do so came from. All I can say is that, at that time, I had only one goal. I was obsessed with only one thing – I had to protect my motherland at any cost. A soldier who has the country's flag and Mother India dwelling in his heart and mind can go to any extent to defend her. At that moment, all he can see is the goal in front of him. Everything else takes a backseat.

***

I was a newly engaged young man of nineteen when I reached Drass with my unit, the 18 Grenadiers regiment, on the 5th of May 1999. As I look back now, at that young age, I not only had the opportunity to fight the war for my country but I was also awarded the Param Vir Chakra, the country's highest military decoration, which was a historic moment in my life. This moment gave a new dimension to my life. Every moment that I spent fighting that war still comes alive before my eyes. I can still see how our brave soldiers not only took back every inch of our motherland from our treacherous neighbours, but also showed the world that no matter what the circumstances, the Indian Army is always ready, prepared, and fully capable of defending its land. We have been taught that we must protect our country and land at any cost, even if we have to sacrifice our lives.

My mind goes back to a particular point during the battle. As I lay injured, the thought that came to my mind was how Bhagat Singh, Rajguru and Sukhdev had sacrificed their lives for the country at such young ages, whereas I, in comparison, had only lost a little blood. Our country has been the land of bravehearts for centuries. In every war, the brave soldiers of India have always staked everything to protect the country. I did not do anything extraordinary; I just followed those high ideals.

Every corner of India resounds with the accounts of many gallant fighters. It makes me very happy that Rishi Raj ji has personally visited all those places, and not only has he paid tribute to the bravehearts, but has also tried to make the readers aware of the history of those places.

We should never forget our heroes. We must always remember that it is because of these lionhearts that we, the Indian citizens, can breathe the air of freedom. The title of this book – The Battlefield Diaries – is eloquent in itself. It introduces us to the heroic deeds of the brave men of our country, and this effort is not only unique but also commendable, for which I congratulate Rishi Raj ji. Today's young generation must read this book and learn about the golden history of war in our country, as well as the places and heroes associated with it. But above all, they must learn about the price that has been paid for the freedom that they enjoy. That debt can never be paid back, but we can fulfil our duty by remembering the heroes and paying homage to them.

Rishi Raj ji started this book with the Revolution of 1857, and has ended with the Kargil War. He covers an entire gamut of the modern history of war in our country. From Mangal Pandey, Bhagat Singh, Udham Singh, Ramprasad 'Bismil', Chandra Shekhar Azad, Somnath Sharma, to Shaitan Singh, Nirmal Jit Singh Sekhon, Arjan Singh, Sam Manekshaw, Manoj Kumar Pandey, Vikram Batra among many other bravehearts and heroes. Rishi Raj ji has brought them together in this book, recalling their valour and selflessness.

I salute all the heroes and bravehearts of our country; I salute their families.

No one can stop a valiant man from fulfilling his mission; No one can kill the one who is unafraid of dying.
Jai Hind!

—Sub Maj (Hon Capt) Yogendra Singh Yadav, PVC

The histo
had to

ages. This st
First, the M
of men and
sacrifices of
and sacrifices
for freedom
their own wa
have differe
objective, a
lives for the
blessed day,
however, w
independen
the same go
goals. As a
I'm sure you

Our las
an example
was making
occupied th
being trounc

PREFACE

The history of our country has been witness to the fact that it has had to struggle to prove its greatness for centuries, or rather, for ages. This struggle did not last for a year or two, but almost 400 years. First, the Mughals invaded us, and then the British ruled us. Thousands of men and women sacrificed their lives in this incessant struggle, the sacrifices of many revolutionaries not even coming to light. Their names and sacrifices have disappeared in the sands of time. In this struggle for freedom at different points in time, everyone fought relentlessly in their own way, with the aim of liberating the country. The methods may have differed, but the objective was the same – freedom. To fulfil this objective, approximately 7.5 lakh brave people willingly sacrificed their lives for the country without giving a thought to their families. Then, on a blessed day, we saw the sun of independence rising. After independence, however, we had to fight people who were part of us till the day before independence. We shared the same heritage, the same language, and also the same goal. But with time, the circumstances changed, and so did the goals. As a result, we found ourselves standing face to face in a stand-off. I'm sure you have guessed whom I'm talking about.

Our last encounter with Pakistan was in Kargil. That war was also an example of an act of treachery. On the one hand, our Prime Minister was making overtures for peace in Lahore, and on the other, Pakistan occupied the Kargil hills. The country refuses to learn a lesson despite being trounced every time. However, the deepest wound was inflicted on us by a country that stabbed us in the back while chanting the slogan '*Bhai-Bhai*'. That sixty-two-year-old wound still haunts us.

However, if we have to begin right at the start, we must go back to the struggle that began in Barrackpore and Meerut in 1857. After that, whether it was the War of Kashmir in 1947, the war with China in 1962, or the wars with Pakistan in 1965, 1971, and again in 1999, our heroes sacrificed themselves unflinchingly. They certainly did everything to protect their country and the people, and no one can ever doubt it. But the question arises – what have we given them in return?

Have we given them the respect they truly deserve? The gratitude for the freedom we enjoy? Often, I feel the answer is no. No, we have not given them what we owe them. More specifically, the newer generations seem to have forgotten these brave men. The only way to prevent this is to make the next generations aware of the chronicles of these great revolutionaries, freedom fighters and bravehearts, along with the places associated with them. I believe they should be taken to pay homage at the places where the bravehearts showed indomitable courage or sacrificed their lives while protecting their motherland.

My only purpose behind writing this book is to introduce today's generation to the architects of India, who protected the country with their blood and created an environment where we live in peace and security today. I believe that, as Indians, we owe a lifetime's debt to these great bravehearts and revolutionaries. We can never repay it in full, but we can definitely lighten it a little by visiting places related to them, meeting their families, and making the younger generations aware of their deeds to keep their memory alive. This is what I have attempted in this book. However, I am neither a historian nor a great scholar. I am just an ordinary person who wants to visit every part of our glorious country and convey its heroic stories to today's young generation.

During this tour, I had the privilege of visiting many such places in India and paying homage to the bravehearts. Through this book, I have made a humble effort to introduce you to the historical importance of those places. I have given information about approximately fifty such places, which are associated with bravehearts and patriots. I hope that this book will be a bridge that will help connect the older generation with today's young generation, and I sincerely hope that it will be made available not only to you, my readers, but to every child of today's generation. All the information contained in this book has been compiled by me with complete honesty and hard labour from available books, the internet, and my own visits to the places. If there is any error in the book, I apologize in advance.

I want neither life nor money,
All I want is for this country to be peaceful.
As long as I live, it will be for this motherland,
And when I die, I desire a Tricolour shroud.
(Unknown)

Dr Rishi Raj

A Note of Appreciation

I am deeply grateful to my parents, whose love and guidance have shaped my life. Their unwavering support and sacrifices are the foundation of who I am today. I extend my heartfelt thanks to my wife, Smt. Sonia Arora, and my beloved children, Niyati and Kartikaye. Their unconditional love and encouragement infuse me with new energy every day. Without their steadfast support, undertaking so many journeys and projects would have been impossible.

I owe a profound debt of gratitude to my mentors and friends from the Indian Army, who have inspired and guided me in numerous ways. My heartfelt thanks to Major Haripal Singh Ahluwalia, Lieutenant General Pitambar Kishor Rampal, Colonel V.N. Thapar (father of Kargil martyr Captain Vijayant Thapar), Colonel Prabhu Raj, Lieutenant Colonel Shashikant Sharma, Major S.P. Singh, Major Nuti Kumar Rathod, Shri K.S. Walia (Ex-IG/BSF), Shri Amar Singh Chauhan (Ex-BSF), and Shri Prabodh Chandra from CISF. Their wisdom and encouragement have been invaluable to my journey.

I sincerely thank Dr Vikas Kumar, MD/DMRC, for his unwavering support and encouragement. I also acknowledge his family's inspiring legacy – his maternal grandfather, the late Shri Malkhan Singh, was a revered freedom fighter from Aligarh. My gratitude extends to my mentors and guide Dr Amit Kumar Jain, Director/Operations, DMRC and a vivid author. Special thanks to Shri Anuj Dayal, Head of Public Relations DMRC.

My sincere thanks to my team member Sonali Dhoundiyal for reading the first draft and giving some valuable suggestions. I am equally grateful to my childhood friend, Shri Gaurav Pathak, and my other friends, Deepak Rajput, Dr Thinlis, Shri Amit Kamra, Shri Ashwani Chawla, and Shri Tarun Malhotra, who accompanied me on meaningful journeys to Kargil and other destinations.

A heartfelt mention goes to my elder brother, Mr Naresh Gulati, who cultivated my love for literature from an early age.

To each of you mentioned above – and to those whose quiet support has been a guiding light – thank you. This book is as much yours as it is mine.

Dr Rishi Raj

1

First War of Independence 1857: The Forerunners

The freedom struggle of 1857 was the first national war that was fought for Swadharma and Swarajya.

—Vinayak Damodar Savarkar

Mangal Pandey's name is etched in golden letters in the history of India. The credit for launching the first armed revolution against the British goes to Mangal Pandey, often called the first freedom fighter of India. Born on 19th July 1827, he sacrificed his life for the country at the young age of twenty-nine.

The British arrived in India in 1600 when they established the East India Company. The company aimed to promote trade between India and England. Gradually, they started to expand their business. They built warehouses and offices in the ports like Calcutta and Surat, among others. Their business started flourishing after the then-Mughal emperor Jahangir gave them the required permits. While in India, the British observed that India was made up of various states, and the kings and leaders were anything but united. Very often, they were at each other's throats. They were all concerned about their own selfish ends and not worried about their subjects' welfare. That is when the British realized that it would not be difficult to rule the country. To achieve this goal, all they had to do was implement the policy of 'Divide and Rule'. They started putting their plan into action. They first started by establishing their dominance in Bengal. Then, by the year 1707, after the death of Aurangzeb, the dominance of the Mughal Sultanate almost came to an end. As the Mughal Sultanate died a slow death, there was no single power that could hold the country together. And this weakness proved to be the strength of the British.

On 23rd June 1757, a battle took place between Nawab Siraj-ud-Daula of Bengal and the British in Plassey near Calcutta. In this war, the British Army was led by Robert Clive. The misgivings regarding the war came true. The British conspired with the three generals of the Nawab's army and a local wealthy merchant. As a result, the Nawab's army could not enter the battle with its full strength and lost. Mir Jafar emerged as the most prominent traitor, and this victory boosted the company's confidence. In 1764, the British also won the Battle of Buxar, thus establishing their supremacy in Bengal. There were many such traitors in the country, too, who could not only commit treason but also go to any extent to satiate their personal greed. These traitors became stooges of the British. They would inform the British of the weaknesses of their rulers to achieve personal gains. History is witness to the fact that these traitors played a major role in dividing the country. This was a good beginning as far as the British were concerned, and it boosted their spirit. Gradually, they began to expand their holdings, and the desire to bring the whole of India under their control arose within them. This went on from 1757 to 1857. That means in those hundred years, the British expanded their presence all over India.

Mangal Pandey, the main protagonist of the armed revolution of 1857, was a soldier in the 34th Bengal Native Infantry of the British Army. He was posted in Barrackpore, Bengal. On 20th March 1857, the soldiers were given new Enfield rifles along with a new gunpowder cartridge, which had to be bitten at one end before use. The main reason for the resentment was that these cartridges were lubricated with cow and pig fat. Mangal Pandey, a Hindu Brahmin, was irked by this. He refused to use those cartridges and conveyed his decision to the British officers. The other comrades in the army also supported Mangal Pandey. In a way, this incident sounded the bugle of India's first war of independence, or it can be said that it turned the smouldering spark of freedom into a burning flame. British historians call this incident a mere mutiny. But as an Indian, I see it as a pure revolution, that is, as India's first attempt to attain freedom. Veer Savarkar, too, considered it as 'the first national struggle for our religion and freedom'.

On 29th March, Mangal Pandey picked up his gun, raised it to his forehead, and called out to his comrades, "Come, the time has come to wipe out the British. Mother India is calling out to you. Arise and destroy these foreigners." Meanwhile, a British sergeant-major named Hewson arrived at the scene. He gave orders to arrest Mangal Pandey. But none of the soldiers obeyed him. A bullet was fired from Mangal Pandey's gun, killing Hewson. Meanwhile, a lieutenant named Baugh arrived there on horseback. Mangal Pandey fired another bullet, which hit Baugh's horse, toppling him. Baugh fired his pistol at Mangal Pandey, but he missed his mark. Mangal Pandey moved with lightning speed and killed Baugh with a sword. He had slayed two British officers. Just then, Colonel Hearsey arrived at the parade ground. But none of the soldiers wanted to lay a hand on Mangal Pandey.

Unfortunately, Mangal Pandey was also injured. After a short while, many British soldiers arrived at the spot. Mangal Pandey, bleeding from his wounds, once again called upon his comrades. His clarion call did not have the desired effect on the other soldiers. They were not driven to take any action, perhaps because some of them thought that the mutiny was going to take place on its fixed date of 31st May. Mangal Pandey placed the gun on his chest and fired as he did not want to be captured alive and tortured by the British. But unfortunately, he survived. He was immediately taken to the military hospital. He was hanged on 8th April 1857.

Barrackpore was the first place to witness the Revolt of 1857, so it is natural that I was very excited when I got a chance to visit the city in 2016.

We took an early morning flight from Delhi. We landed at Kolkata's Netaji Subhash Chandra Bose International Airport and were soon on our way in a taxi to Barrackpore, which was twenty-four kilometres away from Kolkata.

The previous night, my friend, Mahendra Niranjan, had mentioned that his younger brother was a major in the army and was posted in Barrackpore. When I talked to his younger brother, I learnt that the place where Mangal Pandey was hanged was located inside the police academy. The public did not have access to it, though. I also learnt that even before Mangal Pandey, the British had hanged a soldier in the year 1824 for leading his soldiers to revolt against the British on the 1st of November 1824. The feat of the brave soldier named Binda Tiwari was repeated thirty-three years later by Mangal Pandey. It is entirely possible that Binda Tiwari may have been Mangal Pandey's inspiration. It is not as if no revolutions had been attempted before 1857. Attempts had certainly been made. However, those incidents could not convert the spark into a fire because the British Government was able to suppress the efforts with utmost cruelty and intensity.

I came to know about another similar incident when I went to Vellore in Tamil Nadu in 2016. When I visited the Vellore Fort and researched its history, I learnt some startling facts. The bugle of revolution had sounded in Vellore back in 1806. It turns out that two infantry regiments of the Madras Army of the British Government had been stationed there. The soldiers were ordered to wear caps instead of turbans and shave their beards. Apart from this, they were also ordered to put plumes made of cowhide on the cap. This hurt the religious sentiments of the soldiers, and their reaction took a violent turn. The consequence of this revolution was that ten British officers and about a hundred British soldiers were killed.

Although nearly 800 Indian soldiers had been involved in the revolt, they were immediately dispersed, and by the afternoon, the rebellion was crushed. The British Government was, however, stunned by this incident. As a result, the then Governor Lord William Bentinck was summoned back to Britain. Colonel Gillespie, the Commandant of Vellore, quelled the rebellion. However, the flames had spread to three other areas, and the contentious ordinances had to be withdrawn, with the government having to declare that it would not take any actions to hurt the religious sentiments of the soldiers.

It is unfortunate that such an important incident, and factually, the first revolution, has remained buried in the pages of history. The Revolution of 1857 had occupied all the pages of history as the first war against the British, when, in fact, a spark of revolution was lit in India fifty-one years before the revolution of 1857. Apart from this, in 1824, the brave Queen Chennamma of Kittur, Karnataka, raised her voice against the British Government. She was the first female ruler to do so. She won the initial battle but died as a prisoner of war during the next battle.

There was a light drizzle when I reached Barrackpore. First of all, I went to the police academy and paid homage to the memorial built at the site where Mangal Pandey was hanged. This place is surrounded by banyan trees which were silent witnesses to the happenings of that fateful day in history. A noose is shown hanging around the neck of Mangal Pandey's statue. I have not seen such a unique monument anywhere else in the country. After spending some time there, we visited the temple of Binda Tiwari, also located within the precincts of the cantonment area where the public is not allowed. There is an idol of Lord Hanuman in the temple, and there is a small statue of Binda Tiwari wearing an army uniform. The tree from which Binda Tiwari was hanged still stands tall.

Mangal Pandey Udyan is located on the banks of the Hooghly River, where there is a statue of the famous freedom fighter. There, I had an opportunity to chat with Lieutenant Colonel Shashikant Sharma, who, like me, is a resident of Delhi. He said that the Barrackpore Cantonment was the first cantonment established by the British in India, which meant that Barrackpore was the oldest cantonment in India. Also, perhaps this was the only cantonment where some houses and plots had been leased out to commoners. After gathering a lot of interesting information, I took his leave and left for Kolkata. It was indeed a humbling experience to visit a place replete with history.

Less than two months after the revolt in Barrackpore, in the north of the country, on 10th May 1857, the first armed revolution took place in Meerut, Uttar Pradesh, under the leadership of Dhan Singh Gurjar. People from many states in North India eagerly took part in the revolution. On 6th May, the British had given new cartridges to ninety soldiers stationed in the Meerut Cantonment. Out of the ninety, eighty-five soldiers refused to open them. There was a rebellion. The British stripped all those eighty-five soldiers, took away their weapons, and put them in a lock-up. Then, on 10th May, there was a revolt under the leadership of Dhan Singh Gurjar. All the soldiers in captivity were freed. Even today, 10th May is celebrated as Revolution Day. Dhan Singh

Gurjar was publicly hanged by the British at an intersection in Meerut. This incident added fuel to the fire and ignited the flame of mutiny. That is why Meerut was said to be the starting point of the bigger revolution. After this, a chain of revolts against the British started. These incidents shook the British government.

A few leading revolutionaries prepared a draft for a united fight. The chief among them was Nana Saheb, Tatya Tope, Rani Lakshmi Bai and her adviser Lakshman Rao, Kunwar Singh, Rao Tularam, Khan Bahadur Khan, Begum Hazrat Mahal and Bahadur Shah Zafar. They had chosen the of 31st of May for the revolt. But destiny had other plans. Mangal Pandey and the events that unfolded at Meerut had alerted the British, and the collective plans were unsuccessful.

In August 2016, I went to Meerut and had the honour of paying homage to the memorial of the revolutionaries there. It is situated in the yard of the Kali Paltan Temple (Augharnath Shiv Temple) in Meerut. It is said that the water well where the Indian sepoys who fired the first shots assembled still exists there. Apart from this, tanks won in the war with Pakistan are displayed in Meerut Cantonment, along with a national memorial depicting the Revolt of 1857. A political museum built by the Uttar Pradesh Government and a huge statue of Mangal Pandey are reminders of the eventful past of the place.

Their plans may have failed, but these eminent personalities sounded the bugle against British rule in their respective regions of authority. When Peshwa Bajirao II lost the battle of Pune to the British, he went to Bithoor. There, he built a fort for himself and several temples. The British continued to give him a pension of Rs 8,00,000 every year in exchange for the princely state of Pune. Since he did not have a son, he adopted Nana Saheb. Bajirao continued to receive the pension till he was alive. But after his death, the British refused to recognize Nana

Saheb as the successor. They also discontinued the pension. Hence, Nana Saheb revolted against the British. It is interesting that Tatya Tope, Nana Saheb, his elder brother Rao Saheb and Rani Lakshmi Bai spent their childhood together in Bithoor. Under the supervision of Bajirao Peshwa, all four received rigorous training in horse riding and fencing. Later, this training came in handy when they fought for their motherland.

During my visit to Pune, I made a trip to Shaniwarwada, which was once the official residence of Bajirao. Shaniwarwada was built in 1732 for Peshwa Bajirao, the prime minister of the then-Maratha emperor, Chhatrapati Shahu Maharaj. It is a seven-storey building and had cost Rs 16,100 at that time. It was the official residence of Peshwa Bajirao until the British came into power in 1818. After 1818, Bajirao shifted to Bithoor in Uttar Pradesh. Bajirao, who once had a glorious history, decided to first live in Mathura as per his pact with the British, and then went off to Bithoor near Kanpur. Kanpur was another place where Nana Saheb and Tatya Tope challenged the sovereignty of the British and defeated the British Army not only once, but twice. However, the revolutionaries lacked resources. The British Army, on the other hand, had modern weapons. In Bareilly, Khan Bahadur Khan was ousted by the British from power for a short time as well.

Tatya Tope was a brave Maratha warrior. He was born in Yeola, Maharashtra. During the 1857 Rebellion in Kanpur, Tatya Tope, who was a staunch supporter of Nana Saheb, managed to win over the Indian troops of the East India Company. He soon became the commander-in-chief of the rebel forces as the rebellion intensified. An Englishman named Persichros wrote that Tatya had the sharpest mind among the leaders of the Indian rebellion. If there had been more people like him, the rebels could have easily snatched their country away from the

British. Not only Indians but the British were impressed by his bravery as well.

Tatya Tope was betrayed in the Paron forests in Madhya Pradesh. Man Singh, a vassal of the princely state of Narwar in the Gwalior Sultanate, joined forces with the British, leading to Tatya Tope's arrest. He was hanged on 18th April 1859. As he was taken to the gallows, his last words were: *"You may hang me today. But thousands of revolutionaries will arise in my place, and your goal will never be accomplished."* In 2024, I got the chance to visit Shivpuri in Madhya Pradesh, where he was hanged till death.

***

Rani Lakshmi Bai played a key role in the Revolt of 1857. After the mutiny began in Meerut, Lakshmi Bai was proclaimed the ruler of Jhansi. When the British arrived at Jhansi to lay siege over the city, Lakshmi Bai refused to surrender and managed to hold off the East India Company's forces for two weeks. Unfortunately, they were greatly outnumbered, and finally, the city fell. The queen had to leave Jhansi because of the traitors in her army. Rani Lakshmi Bai escaped to Kalpi and later to Gwalior. At Gwalior, Lakshmi Bai continued to fight alongside leaders like Tatya Tope and Nana Saheb. She died heroically fighting the British till her last breath and became a martyr on 18th June 1858.

A *samadhi* has been built at the place where Rani of Jhansi attained martyrdom in the Phool Bagan complex in Gwalior. The place is no less than a site of pilgrimage. Among the valiant women of India, no other woman has been accorded the position that the Rani of Jhansi has attained. There is no Indian who is not aware of the bravery of the queen of Jhansi; children read about her in school today. So, how could

I remain untouched? In August 2019, I visited her samadhi with my family to pay my respects. A few years earlier, in February 2013, I also had the privilege of visiting her fort in Jhansi. The fort stands atop a hill in the centre of the city. It was the prime centre of the clashes between the British and the rebels during the mutiny. Rani Lakshmi Bai escaped by jumping from the fort onto her horse. The spot where she jumped is now known as the Jumping Point. It was quite humbling to be present at a spot where history had witnessed such important events.

Apart from the rather well-known revolutionaries I have spoken about, there were many others who took part in India's First War of Independence from different parts of the country:

1. Kanpur – Nana Saheb and Tatya Tope
2. Bareilly – Khan Bahadur Khan Rohila
3. Satara – Rangoji Bapu
4. Gorakhpur – Gajodhar Singh
5. Kullu – Rana Pratap Singh and Veer Singh
6. Jagdishpur, Bihar – Kunwar Singh and Amar Singh
7. Sagar – Sheikh Ramzan
8. Faizabad – Maulvi Ahmadullah
9. Haryana – Rao Tularam
10. Sultanpur – Shahid Hassan
11. Mathura – Devi Singh
12. Mandsaur – Shahzada Feroz Shah
13. Raipur – Narayan Singh
14. Assam – Maniram Dewan
15. Allahabad – Liyaqat Ali
16. Sambalpur, Odisha – Rajkumar Surendra Sahi and Ujjwal Sahi

The history of India cannot be imagined without talking about all these bravehearts who took part in the first fight for freedom. Though the rebellion was squashed, it had rattled the British. During the initial years of the 1857 revolution, the British Government sentenced about 4,000 revolutionaries to the infamous Kala Pani prison in the Andaman and Nicobar islands. It was a message from the British Government to the public that whoever raised a voice against the British would face the same consequences.

But how could those who were obsessed with liberating the country remain silent?

Around 1870, the embers of the revolution were rekindled again. A revolutionary from Pune raised his voice against the British Empire. He was Vasudev Balwant Phadke. He was born on 4th November 1845 in the Raigarh district of Maharashtra. He got a government job at the young age of fifteen. One day, he received a letter about his mother's illness. He immediately approached the British officer to ask for leave but was met with discourtesy as he was Indian. The officer first delayed in granting him leave and later refused to do so. Phadke still went ahead, but by the time he reached home, he found that his mother had passed away. This incident shook him to the core, and he decided to take a strong stand against British rule. He gathered the Ramoshi tribals and formed an armed group. They launched violent attacks, and the British were terrified of the group, which operated in seven districts of Maharashtra.

Eventually, the British arrested him and sent him to a jail in Yemen. It is said that he went on a hunger strike there and passed away shortly in February 1883.

His memorial is located near Pune station. At the entrance is the bust of Phadke on a cement concrete cave. Just a few steps away is the building where the trial of Phadke and his men was held in the year 1879. During my visit to Pune in June 2016, I had the good fortune of visiting his memorial and paying my homage to a martyr who made an unforgettable contribution to the freedom movement. Vasudev Balwant Phadke became an abiding role model for the revolutionaries of Maharashtra.

In 1871, the Namdhari Sikhs in Punjab also launched a movement against the British. The Namdhari Sikhs protested against the slaughterhouses that were being opened by the British at various locations and carried out an armed revolution against them, in which sixty-six Namdhari Sikhs were martyred. This entire movement was led by Satguru Ram Singh. The sacrifice of these Namdhari Sikhs cannot be consigned to oblivion as it was an important part of the initial rebellions against British rule.

A few years later, towards the end of 1896, a dreadful plague broke out in Maharashtra. The British Government sent a British officer named Walter Charles Rand to Pune to contain it. Rand dealt with the citizens there in a very contemptible manner. His conduct angered the three Chapekar brothers from Maharashtra – Damodar, Balkrishna and Vasudev Chapekar. The three brothers planned the assassination of a British officer. On the birth anniversary of Shivaji Maharaj, the Chapekar brothers appealed to all Marathas to recall the valour of heroic Shivaji and made them remember the promise of liberating the country from the British. In 1897, the British Government commemorated sixty years of the reign of the Queen of England. It was celebrated all over India. When Rand was returning from the celebrations in Pune, the Chapekar brothers jumped on his carriage from behind, shot him, and fled from the scene. Rand died on the spot. The assassination had gone as planned, but the three brothers were soon arrested. Damodar Chapekar was hanged on 18th April 1898, Balkrishna Chapekar on 12th May 1899 and Vasudev Chapekar on 8th May 1899. This was the first and last incident in the history of India's freedom struggle, where all the sons of a mother happily gave up their lives for the country. The country can never forget the sacrifice made by the Chapekar brothers.

Notable events took place in 1907 in London. On the one hand, the British Government was celebrating fifty years after the failure of India's First War of Independence, and on the other hand, India's famous nationalist, Veer Savarkar, was camping at Shyamji Krishna Varma's India House in London. He continuously brought together those who were working towards India's independence. Veer Savarkar was irked that the British Government mocked the First War of Independence of 1857. The British Government even staged plays in which Nana Saheb, Tatya Tope and Rani Lakshmi Bai were portrayed as rebels, and their martyrdom was derided. Indian revolutionaries, on the other hand, celebrated the Golden Jubilee of the First Indian War of Independence at India House on 10th May 1907 and demonstrated that the struggle of 1857 was not a rebellion but India's first freedom struggle. They decided to celebrate it as a memorable anniversary. Shining badges were specially prepared for this, and during the celebration, all the revolutionaries pinned them on their chests and proudly displayed them.

During his stay in Britain, Veer Savarkar quietly immersed himself in the study of the freedom struggle of 1857 in the London library for several months. He realized that to keep the flame of revolution burning, the people would have to be made aware of the efforts made in 1857, or else people would forget the sacrifices made by Nana Saheb, Tatya Tope and Rani Lakshmi Bai, among others, which would result in the weakening of the struggle for freedom. And that could never be allowed to happen.

Savarkar penned a book which, even before it was published, was banned by the British Government. But for our revolutionaries, it was akin to the *Gita*. Every revolutionary was secretly given that book to read so they could learn what role the revolutionaries played in the struggle for freedom of 1857 and so that they could draw inspiration from it. The title of this book was '1857 *ka Swatantrya Samar*'. No one had imagined that a book would frighten the British Government so much. The book was printed in Holland, and copies of it were sent secretly to France and then to other places. In 1910, Veer Savarkar was arrested and sentenced to the infamous Kala Pani prison.

Veer Savarkar''s full name was Vinayak Damodar Savarkar. He was born on 28th May 1883 in Bhagur, Nasik. In June 2016, I had the honour of going there and paying obeisance. A museum has been built at his birthplace. Bhagur is adjacent to the Deoli military cantonment. After travelling for about half an hour from Nashik, crossing the cantonment area, and then walking through some alleys, I reached the hallowed place along with my family. The museum has a ground floor and a first floor. Many old photographs displayed there recount the sacrifices and the fearless efforts made by Veer Savarkar to liberate the country.

Once during my visit to Mumbai, I had an opportunity to visit his memorial located opposite Shivaji Park. Spread over an area of 6,650 square metres, this memorial was inaugurated on 28th May 1989 by the then President, Dr Shankar Dayal Sharma. There is a library inside this memorial where children are given training in boxing, judo, shooting and many other sports. It also has a model of Jail No. 123 of Kala Pani, where Veer Savarkar was imprisoned.

Back to the forerunners, along with various individuals and groups in India, efforts to liberate the country have intensified in foreign countries, too. Shyamji Krishna Varma worked to unite the Indian revolutionaries in London. Shyamji Krishna Varma was born on 4th October 1857 in Mandvi, Gujrat. He became the first Indian to receive an MA and a Bar at Law degree from Oxford University. Later, he joined the university as a professor of Sanskrit. As I mentioned earlier, he founded India House in London, where he brought together nationalists like Veer Savarkar, Madanlal Dhingra, Madam Bhikaji Cama and others. During my journey to London in 2018, I made a point to visit India House to see the place which played a key role in bringing the revolutionaries together. In 1905, he started publishing a monthly newspaper called *The Indian Sociologist*. Shyamji Krishna Varma passed away in 1930 in Geneva. But his last wish was that his ashes be taken to India after the country gained independence.

During my trip to Kutch in March 2016, Mandvi remained in my thoughts. Earlier, all I knew about Mandvi was that the beach there was worth visiting and that the sunsets were spectacular. When Narendra Modi became the prime minister of the country in 2014, he spoke about Shyamji Krishna Varma. That aroused my curiosity, and when I learnt that Mandvi is the hallowed place where the great revolutionary was born, I knew a visit was on the cards during our tour of Kutch. When he was the Chief Minister of Gujarat in 2003, Prime Minister Narendra Modi went to Geneva, where Varma passed away in 1930. He brought his ashes back to Mandvi. They were kept at Kranti Teerth, the museum that was built at his birthplace in his honour, which I had the honour of visiting in March 2016. Kranti Teerth is a replica of India House. Shyamji Krishna Varma's ashes remain there, and information about other revolutionaries is also available, making sure the sacrifices of these brave men are never forgotten.

The martyrdom of the revolutionaries started bearing fruit. Apart from India and London, revolutionaries had also started to converge in America and Canada to liberate India. Two men in particular gained prominence and became part of this movement – Lala Hardayal and

Sohan Singh Bhakna. In 1913, they founded the Ghadar Party together with Kartar Singh Sarabha, Maulvi Barkatullah, Rash Behari Bose and other revolutionaries in California. The party's goal was to overthrow British rule in India, and it published a weekly newspaper that spread its message of revolution to Indian immigrants all over the world. In the year 2024, I got an opportunity to visit the Gadar Memorial built in San Francisco, USA. It is currently being maintained by the Ministry of External Affairs, Government of India.

In 1914, Bhagat Singh's father, Sardar Kishan Singh, donated Rs 1,000 to the Ghadar Party. Bhagat Singh was greatly influenced by Kartar Singh Sarabha, who was an active member of the Ghadar Party. Bhagat Singh considered Sarabha as his model and always carried his photograph with him. Then arose a storm when fifty-five revolutionaries of the Ghadar Party were hanged at the same time by the British Government. The most prominent among them was Kartar Singh Sarabha, who went to the gallows with a smile at the mere age of nineteen. Many of his comrades were sent to Kala Pani. The Ghadar Rebellion was unsuccessful. However, it helped to raise awareness of the Indian independence movement and inspired future generations of revolutionaries.

Going back to the revolt in Meerut on 10th May 1857, the rebel soldiers raised the slogan *'Dilli Chalo'* simultaneously, and everyone immediately began marching towards Delhi. The soldiers reached Delhi on 11th May.

The soldiers crossed the Yamuna over a bridge of boats. Unlike Meerut, there were no military cantonments in Delhi at that time. The cantonment was in a nearby village called Rajpur, where the North Campus of Delhi University is now located. A street named Rajpur Road exists even today. As the revolting soldiers arrived, the families of British soldiers took refuge in the Flagstaff Tower, which was a signal tower. The Flagstaff Tower tells its history in the Ridge Garden of Delhi University, even today. A street named after it is called Flagstaff Road. Currently, the chief minister of Delhi lives on the road. On 11th May, after a day-long horrific carnage, the revolutionaries proclaimed Mughal Emperor Bahadur Shah Zafar II as their leader.

The British called their army from Ambala, Punjab and Meerut. The revolutionaries and British soldiers clashed at many places in Delhi. On 8th June, a fierce battle took place at Badli ki Sarai in Delhi, where the British Army came face-to-face with rebel soldiers. The soldiers fought valiantly but were defeated by the tactical skills of the British. Major General Sir Henry Bernard had specially arrived from Haryana's Karnal to help the army contingent, which was led by Major Wilson. About three hundred rebel soldiers and British soldiers were killed in this ferocious battle. Even today, two buildings standing opposite each other tell the story of this battle. This place was once an inn where travellers used to rest. Only two entrances of the building are left now. That is why the colony here was named Sarai Peepal Thala, which still exists on GT Karnal Road in North Delhi. This historical place is hardly 200 meters from the Adarsh Nagar Metro Station.

Finally, by 20th September 1857, Delhi was recaptured by the British. The objective of the sepoys to name Bahadur Shah Zafar as the Emperor of India remained unfulfilled. He was apprehended and banished to Rangoon in Burma, where he died. His words as he was banished:

"दमदमे में दम नहीं है, अब खैर मांगो जान की ..."

Delhi is peppered with monuments and remains that remind the present residents of its past. The Ajitgarh Memorial, formerly known as the Mutiny Memorial, was built in 1863 in memory of the British soldiers who died during the revolution of 1857. A red sandstone tower built in Gothic design, it is a 29.5 metre-high tower. A stone in the memorial has the number of British officers and soldiers who died in the mutiny. In 1972, during the 25th anniversary of India's independence, the Indian government renamed the monument Ajitgarh or the 'Place of the Unvanquished.' It was also mentioned that the 'enemy' on the memorial were the 'immortal martyrs for Indian freedom', signifying the bravery of these early revolutionaries.

The Red Fort is another monument that became a symbol for the sepoys when they declared Bahadur Shah Zafar as their leader. Though none of the battles took place at the fort in 1857, after the British quelled the rebellion, they took over the Red Fort. Most of the marble structures were demolished, and a garrison was built inside the complex. Interestingly, there are four museums inside the fort, which are maintained by the Archaeological Survey of India. Two of them are the Freedom Struggle Museum and the Freedom Fighter Museum, where the weapons used during the revolution of 1857 are displayed.

The Red Fort is one of the most historically significant structures in the history of India. When the country gained independence on 15th August 1947, the tricolour was hoisted here for the first time. Even today, every year, the prime minister addresses the nation from the ramparts of the Red Fort. The fluttering tricolour takes us back to history and constantly reminds us of our glorious past and bravehearts. The Red Fort is a glowing symbol of our independence and national pride.

Close to the Kashmere Gate Metro Station is the Nicholson Cemetery, where many British officers who were killed during the 1857 revolution are buried. This cemetery is named after Brigadier General Nicholson, who was killed during the 1857 revolution and was laid to rest. Kashmere Gate was one of the main centres of the revolutionaries, and many bloody battles took place there. In 1857, a part of it was broken and damaged during an attack by the British Army.

Delhi, especially North Delhi, became the key centre of this revolution. During this period, the biggest carnage was carried out by British General William Hudson. He shot dead three princes of the Mughal Sultanate – Bahadur Shah Zafar's sons Mirza Mughal and Mirza Khizr Sultan and grandson Mirza Abu Bakht. They were shot from inside a building located in front of Ferozeshah Kotla ground near Delhi Gate. After this massacre, it came to be known as Khooni Darwaza.

Some people do not consider the revolution of 1857 successful. But the truth is that the revolution of 1857 became the robust foundation for the core campaign to liberate our country. Even though this revolution was heralded on the grounds of religious faith, the revolutionaries who sacrificed their lives for the country with a smile will be the biggest inspiration for the coming generations. The statement of Veer Savarkar is unequivocally true that the rebellion of 1857 was the first national war fought for *swadharma* and *swarajya*.

2

The Fearless Trio – Shaheed-E-Azam Bhagat Singh, Rajguru and Sukhdev

सरफ़रोशी की तमन्ना अब हमारे दिल में है
देखना है ज़ोर कितना बाज़ू-ए-क़ातिल में है

The city of Ferozepur in Punjab lies on the banks of the mighty Sutlej river. In the last twenty years, I have visited the city twice. My second visit came about in 2016. My kids were teenagers then, and I felt it was the ideal time to sow the seeds of patriotism in them by showing them places of historical and national interest.

The second reason was that through my book, I wanted to inspire today's young generation to visit these sites. The third and last reason was the posting of my friend Lieutenant Colonel Prabhu Raj at Ferozepur, as it is always a more cherished experience to visit a military area with a military officer.

On 24th March 2016, we began our journey from Delhi to Ferozepur. It was a long drive of more than 400 kilometres. We reached our destination in the afternoon and made our way to the guest house in the army cantonment. My friend Prabhu had boating on the Sutlej at the top of our itinerary for us. At 4 p.m., my family and I accompanied Prabhu to the Hussainiwala Sailing Club of the Indian Army. From there, we got into an Indian Army boat. The water of the Sutlej was sheer green and clear. I was amazed at how the water of a river that has travelled

2,000 kilometres could be so clean. The Beas River meets the Sutlej at a place called Harike in the Kapurthala district, which is a few kilometres away from Ferozepur.

In 2012, during my Kailash Manasarovar yatra, I had the opportunity to behold Rakshas Tal, the source of Sutlej. It is said that Ravana did *tapasya* for Lord Shiva for many years while standing in the water on one leg at this very place. That is why this place was named Rakshas Tal. Incidentally, it is also said that the water of Rakshas Tal became salty due to Ravana's many years of tapasya. Kailash Mansarovar region falls in Tibet, and apart from Sutlej, three other rivers originate from here. They are the Sindhu, Karnali and the Brahmaputra. On the other hand, Sutlej enters India from Tibet through Shipki La in Himachal Pradesh and Beas and Sutlej converge in the Kapurthala district of Punjab. After this, Sutlej enters Pakistan from Ferozepur.

It was a wonderful experience to sail on the mighty river. There was a time when Sutlej used to flow right next to Hussainiwala station. Now, it has moved away a little. When I told Prabhu about the history of the Sutlej during sailing, he was astonished. 'Punjab' means five rivers: Sutlej, Ravi, Beas, Chenab, and Jhelum. Sutlej is the longest among them, and it was in this river that the remains of Bhagat Singh, Rajguru and Sukhdev were thrown by the British.

After boating in the Sutlej, we arrived at the Hussainiwala border, which is just half a kilometre from the Martyrs Memorial. Martyrs Memorial in Hussainiwala is the place where the last rites of Bhagat Singh, Rajguru and Sukhdev were performed. Just like the ceremony at the Attari border, a grand ceremony takes place every day at the Hussainiwala border as well, during which soldiers of both countries lower the flags of their respective countries.

Before the 1971 war, this was an open border where trade took place without any restrictions. Compared to the Attari border, this area saw more traffic. In those days, Ferozepur was a radiant and lively city and a major centre of trade. Secondly, the Punjab Mail, which was the most famous train in undivided India, used to start from Peshawar and go to Bombay (present-day Mumbai) via Lahore, Ferozepur, and Delhi. This train was started in 1912 to transport British military officers who arrived from Europe from Bombay to Peshawar.

Now the question that arises is, when Bhagat Singh, Rajguru and Sukhdev were hanged in Lahore jail, how were they cremated in Hussainiwala? There is a story behind this. The 24th of March 1931 was supposed to be the date for hanging the three of them. But lest the public get angry, the three sons of Mother India – Bhagat Singh, Rajguru and Sukhdev were secretly hanged on 23rd March 1931, at around 7:33 p.m. Before going to the gallows, Bhagat Singh was reading a book by Lenin. When the jail authorities informed him that it was time for his execution, he said, "Wait! Let one revolutionary meet another revolutionary first."

After a minute, he tossed the book towards the ceiling and said, "Fine, let's go now."

On the way to the gallows, all three of them sang joyfully:

"Mera rang de basanti chola, mera rang de; mera rang de basanti chola. Maye rang de basanti chola… "

Dreading that a riot might break out after the executions, the jail authorities first chopped their dead bodies into pieces, then packed them in sacks and took them to Hussainiwala, where they set the bodies on fire by pouring kerosene on them instead of ghee. When the people of the village saw the fire burning, they drew closer. Frightened, the British threw the half-burnt pieces of the dead bodies into the Sutlej

River and ran away. But the local people got wind of it, and their mortal remains were not only pulled out of the river but were also cremated with full honour.

Hussainiwala village was earlier with Pakistan. Taking into account the sentiments of Indians, in 1961, the Indian Government gave away twelve villages of Fazilka to Pakistan and took this sacred land in return. In 1968, the construction of the Martyrs Memorial was completed. Pakistani soldiers vandalized this memorial during the 1971 war and also took away with them the statues of the three bravehearts. Owing to the efforts of the then Chief Minister of Punjab, Giani Zail Singh, the dignity of the Martyrs Memorial was restored in 1973.

Apart from Bhagat Singh, Rajguru and Sukhdev, there are two more samadhis. The fourth samadhi is of Batukeshwar Dutt, who was Bhagat Singh's comrade. In 1965, the last rites of Batukeshwar Dutt were performed at this place as per his wish. Batukeshwar Dutt was with Bhagat Singh when he threw a bomb at the Central Assembly. The fifth samadhi is of the late Vidyavatiji, mother of Bhagat Singh. She is known as the 'Mother of Punjab'. Her last wish was that her last rites be performed by her son's samadhi.

In June 1975, her last rites were performed as she had wished. Vidyavatiji had not borne an ordinary child but a hero. Even though Bhagat Singh is not physically present among us today, as long as this universe exists, we will carry his memory like a fragrance in our hearts. During the last meeting, Bhagat Singh told his mother, "After my execution, do not come to collect my dead body; send Kulbir (Bhagat Singh's younger brother) instead," and he roared with laughter.

He added, "Mother, in case you come, you will cry, and if people see you crying, they will say, 'Look, Bhagat Singh's mother is crying.'"

Never will the world see such a brave mother and a lion-like son again! Every year on Martyr's Day, the 23rd of March, a fair is organized at this location and thousands of people gather and pay tribute to the martyrs. Shri Rajiv Gandhi was the first prime minister to visit this memorial; he visited it in the year 1985. Prime Minister Shri Narendra Modi visited it in 2015 and paid tribute to the martyrs.

The remains of the Hussainiwala station are close to the site of the Martyrs Memorial. The remains of Hussainiwala station narrate its golden history. The station master's room, ticket office, and railway tracks exist even today. When the Punjab Mail gloriously swung through Hussainiwala, people's faces would flush with excitement. The station bustled with activity the most during the arrival of this train. Police presence was also highest during this time because the train was filled with British officers. After Independence, Hussainiwala station became deserted; it became the last station of the Northern Railways. Twice a year, on Baisakhi and Shaheed Diwas, the Ferozepur Division of Northern Railways runs a special train between Ferozepur and Hussainiwala so that its history is not forgotten.

Coming back to the bravehearts, there would hardly be anyone in India who is not familiar with the martyrdom of Bhagat Singh, Rajguru and Sukhdev. And why wouldn't everyone be familiar with them? Such great revolutionaries will never be born again. Sardar Bhagat Singh, who went to the gallows at the age of twenty-three, was born in Banga village, Lyallpur of Punjab, which is now in Pakistan. Bhagat Singh was deeply imbued with patriotism since childhood, and it was natural because his grandfather, Arjun Singh, father, Kishan Singh and uncles, Ajit Singh and Swaran Singh, were engaged in the country's freedom struggle for many years.

Bhagat Singh's father had provided a lot of financial support to Lala Lajpat Rai and the Ghadar Party. During his childhood, Bhagat Singh met Kartar Singh Sarabha, who was an active member of the Ghadar Party. Bhagat Singh was so impressed by him and his patriotism that he carried his photo in his pocket at all times and started considering him as his model. He considered everything that Sarabha said to be his creed. Kartar Singh Sarabha was executed by the British Government at the young age of nineteen. Bhagat Singh adopted his principles and resolved to sacrifice his life for the liberation of the country. Once, during his childhood, he was working in the fields. His father, Kishan Singh, asked, "Bhagat, what are you doing?" He replied, "I am sowing guns so that many guns will grow in the fields, and then we will be able to fight the British." Since childhood, he yearned to liberate his motherland.

On 13th April 1919, the Jallianwala Bagh massacre took place, in which British officer Dyer had unarmed Indians gunned down. This heinous massacre shook the entire country. It also deeply affected the young Bhagat Singh. The very next day, Bhagat Singh went to Amritsar from Lahore, brought back the blood-soaked soil from Jallianwala Bagh in a bottle, and vowed that one day he would definitely take revenge on the British. When Gandhiji withdrew his non-cooperation movement in 1920, young Bhagat Singh was heartbroken because he had had a lot of expectations from Gandhiji.

He soon realized that in order to liberate the country, he would have to do something which would create fear in the British Government. At DAV College in Lahore, where he enrolled himself, he came across Sukhdev Thapar, who, like Bhagat Singh, was also very patriotic. Bhagat Singh was very bright in studies. He was deeply interested in studying English, Urdu, and history and had a very good grasp of these subjects. Apart from this, he was also particularly interested in theatre. Through plays, he awakened the spirit of fighting for freedom among the youth. Around this time, he went to Kanpur. There, he started writing for Ganesh Shankar Vidyarthi's Hindi weekly *Pratap*. Before that, he earned his living by selling newspapers, where he met Hindustan Socialist Republican Association members Chandra Shekhar Azad, Ram Prasad Bismil, Batukeshwar Dutt, Manmath Nath Gupta and Ashfaq Ullah Khan. These meetings gave new direction to the life of Bhagat Singh and the freedom struggle.

The association undertook a big task, which was to loot the government treasury at the Kakori station. It was not a robbery. Rather, it was an exciting chapter in the Indian revolutionary movement. The incident took place on 9th August 1925. There is a station called Kakori, which is a short distance from Lucknow. At this station, three youths, Ashfaq Ullah Khan, Sachindra Bakshi and Rajendra Lahiri, boarded a second-class compartment of the Number 8 Down passenger train. The remaining seven members of the team, Ram Prasad Bismil, Keshav Chakraborty, Murari Lal, Mukundi Lal, Banwari Lal, Manmath Nath Gupta and Chandra Shekhar Azad, boarded the third-class compartment of the same train. According to the plan, Rs 4,500, which was being taken to the government treasury, was looted. During the action, a passenger was accidentally killed. Roshan Singh, Ashfaq Ullah Khan, Ram Prasad Bismil and Rajendra Lahiri were given death sentences.

After Bhagat Singh joined the Hindustan Socialist Republican Association, the flame of the freedom struggle, which had been flickering until then, started to burn intensely. In 1926, Bhagat Singh, Bhagwati Charan Vohra, and Yashpal, among others, founded the Naujawan Bharat Sabha.

When the Simon Commission arrived in Lahore in 1928, it was strongly opposed under the leadership of Lala Lajpat Rai. During this protest, British officers lathi-charged Lalaji, due to which he suffered serious injuries. This lathi charge was executed at the orders of British police officer Scott. The injuries were so grievous that Lalaji died ten days later.

There was a wave of strong reaction to this brutality throughout the country. Lala Lajpat Rai wished that the following lines should be taught to every child in India:

मेरा मजहब हक़ परस्ती है,
मेरी मिल्लत कौम परस्ती है।

To avenge the murder of Lala Lajpat Rai, Bhagat Singh, teaming up with Rajguru, killed J.P. Saunders, a British police officer who was the assistant superintendent of police, in Lahore on 17th December 1928. However, their target was Scott, who was the superintendent of police, and Bhagat Singh was quite remorseful about it. This incident shook the British Government to its core. Chandra Shekhar Azad had rendered all help to Bhagat Singh, and he was sent to Calcutta from Lahore with the help of Durga Bhabhi, a female revolutionary, who posed as his wife to help him escape the police. Disguised as an officer, Bhagat Singh took Durga Bhabhi and her son Shachi with him as his family and Rajguru as his servant. Durga Bhabhi's husband, Bhagwati Charan Vohra, was also a great revolutionary who later died on the spot when one of the bombs suddenly exploded during testing.

In Calcutta, Bhagat Singh met Jatin Das, under whom he trained to make bombs. Initially, Jatin Das was hesitant to help the revolutionaries, but Bhagat Singh persuaded him and devoted his life to the service of Mother India. While staying in Lahore jail with Bhagat Singh, Jatin Das went on a hunger strike for more than two months, during which he passed away. During my visit to Calcutta, I saw the intersection named after Bhagat Singh. There is a park named Jatin Das as well. It is said that when Jatin's mortal remains were brought to Calcutta after his martyrdom, about five lakh people attended his funeral, which is a staggering record.

In 1929, to make the British Government take notice, Bhagat Singh decided to blast bombs and distribute pamphlets in the Central Assembly. The 8th of April 1929 was chosen for this. Batukeshwar Dutt was chosen with Bhagat Singh to execute this plan. A room was rented in Kucha Sitaram near Chawri Bazaar in Delhi. Two days before the execution of the plan, Bhagat Singh was photographed wearing a hat at the Ramnath Studio in Kashmere Gate, Delhi. The intention was that when Bhagat's picture would be published in the newspapers, people would take inspiration from him. It is important to mention that the public's perception of the revolutionaries was that they were violent and dangerous, whereas the ground reality was far different.

Finally, the day arrived when Bhagat Singh and all the members of the Hindustan Socialist Republican Association were successful in making the people hear their voices. After throwing a bomb in the Central Assembly, they raised slogans of '*Inquilab Zindabad*, Down with Imperialism!', threw the pamphlets they had brought with them up in the air, and got themselves arrested. Suddenly, the young man wearing a hat who had taken on the British Government in such a fearless way started being discussed throughout the country.

As a matter of fact, this bomb was set off so that the policies being drafted by the British against Indian labourers could be thwarted. When mill workers across the country learnt about this, they also joined forces with Bhagat Singh. This was also the time when the country's politics was divided into two groups – the Moderates and Radicals. On the one hand, the Moderates wanted to achieve independence only by holding protests and preaching about non-violence, while on the other hand, there was a group of Radicals, including Bhagat Singh, Chandra Shekhar Azad, Rajguru, Sukhdev, Ramprasad Bismil, Bal Gangadhar Tilak, Lala Lajpat Rai and Bipin Chandra Pal. They believed that the country could be liberated only when the British Government was taught a lesson and that on this path, they would have to resort to violence. Now, the country had two leaders – one was Mahatma Gandhi, and the other was Bhagat Singh. The latter, a tall and handsome young man, had become a role model for the youth of the country.

After their arrest in October 1930, Bhagat Singh, Rajguru and Sukhdev were sentenced to death in the Lahore Conspiracy Case. When Bhagat Singh was told that he had been sentenced to death, he recited these lines by Kabir:

जिस मरनै थै जग डरै, सो मेरे आनंद।
कब मरिहूँ कब देखिहूँ, पूरन परमानंद।

(That is, even if the world is afraid of death, I will be happy because when death comes to one while walking on the path of right, that perfect bliss is like reaching God.)

And then the ill-fated day of 23rd March 1931 arrived when the three sons of Mother India – Bhagat Singh, Rajguru and Sukhdev were executed. There is nothing more admirable than facing the gallows with a smile at the mere age of twenty-three. There is no doubt that Bhagat Singh is considered the greatest and most respected among the revolutionaries who liberated India. These words of Shaheed Bhagat Singh still echo in the ears of every Indian:

"I will climb the gallows gladly and show to the world how bravely the revolutionaries can sacrifice themselves for the cause."

***

After paying obeisance at the Martyrs Memorial, we proceeded to the Barki War Memorial. A tank seized during the war with Pakistan is kept there. In 1965, when the Indian Army made inroads into Lahore in Pakistan, it also brought back a milestone from there as a souvenir which can be seen there. On one hand, this memorial celebrates the glory of the Indian Army and makes every Indian proud of it. On the other hand, it inspires us to salute the brave soldiers of the Indian Army with respect. Heartfelt salutations to those heroes.

During that trip, we made our way to Khatkad Kalan to see Bhagat Singh's ancestral house and museum. Khatkad Kalan is known as Shaheed Bhagat Singh Nagar. Visiting it is no less than undertaking a pilgrimage. It was a very emotional moment for me when I saw the cot, utensils, cupboards, and other items he used in his house. There is a well in the courtyard of the house. In one corner, the *chulha,* on which the women in the family made rotis, has been preserved.

About a kilometre from Bhagat Singh's ancestral home is a museum dedicated to Bhagat Singh, Rajguru and Sukhdev, in which many items associated with their lives have been preserved, such as books, letters written in their handwriting, newspapers stained with blood, their horoscopes, several photographs of their family members and other revolutionaries. The pen with which the death sentence was written is diplayed, as well as the ashes and fragments of the bones of these young men.

In 2009, the Punjab Government had planned to make this museum world-class; that plan is yet to be implemented. In this regard, I have written a request to the Punjab and Central governments as this is not just a museum but a hallowed place which tells the story of the sacrifice of these mighty bravehearts. After seeing all of this, my respect for Bhagat Singh increased manifold, and I pledged to accomplish something during my lifetime that would help the new generation learn as much as possible about Bhagat Singh and other martyrs, and apply their ideals in their lives. Bhagat Singh often used to hum these lines:

सेवा देश दी जिंदिये बढ़ी औखी,
गल्लां करनियां ढेर सुखाय्यिन ने।
जीना देश सेवा विच पैर पाया,
ओहना लाख मुसीबतां झल्लिया ने।

(That is, it is very easy to talk about serving the country, but it is very difficult to serve the country. Any person who has set foot on the path of serving the country has had to face millions of troubles.)

I consider myself fortunate that in June 2016, I had the opportunity to visit Rajguru Nagar, the birthplace of Shaheed Rajguru, about forty kilometres away from Pune in Maharashtra. His birthplace has been converted into a small museum. The guard showed us the place where he hid his weapons, his place of worship, and also the entrance with a secret passage to escape from the British. There is also the soil from the samadhi of the three patriots kept in a small urn. A lamp burns continuously in front of Rajguru's photograph. I felt at peace as I stood there, recalling the immense sacrifice of the young man.

After paying obeisance at the birthplaces of Bhagat Singh and Rajguru, the next stop was the famous Chaura Bazaar of Ludhiana. There is a place called Nau Ghara, where mainly people from the Thapar community live. This is where Sukhdev's ancestral house is located. In July 2016, I reached the house early in the morning with my friend

Paramjeet. Only after paying obeisance to that piece of land and the house built on it, I felt at peace. The trips to the holy birthplaces of these three martyrs were no less than pilgrimages for me. I was humbled and felt a strange kind of contentment.

Another name that shines like a pole star or the *dhruv tara* in the freedom struggle is Chandra Shekhar Azad. He was a great revolutionary. His dedication and passion for freedom inspired countless people to participate in the freedom struggle. He was born in Jhabua, Madhya Pradesh, on 23rd July 1906 to Pandit Sitaram Tiwari and Jagrani Devi. His original name was Chandra Shekhar Tiwari. He fought fiercely with the British at every opportunity and played an active role in the killing of Saunders and in the Kakori incident. I had the opportunity to visit Alfred Park (now Chandrashekhar Park) in Prayagraj, where I could pay homage to his life-size statue. The visit to the birthplace of Chandra Shekhar Azad, which is in Bhavra, Madhya Pradesh was equally rewarding. In 2018, 2021 and 2024, I had the privilege to visit Satar near Orcha in Madhya Pradesh. There is a small Ashram where Chandra Shekhar Azad had lived in disguise for a few years.

In 2016, the country celebrated the 70th anniversary of Independence. On this occasion, the central government pays a true tribute to the bravehearts by organizing special programmes at various memorials and sites. Prime Minister Narendra Modi himself launched this drive by visiting the birthplace of Chandra Shekhar Azad. He was the first prime minister to visit Azad's birthplace and pay tribute to him. His actions cannot be commended enough because they inspire the younger generation to visit these places and remember the bravehearts.

3

Captives of Kala Pani: Heroes in Prison

मत कहो इसको काला पानी,
तुम सुनो यहाँ की धरती के
कण-कण से गाथा बलिदानी।

In the winter of 2012, we decided to go to the Andaman and Nicobar Islands. The infamous Kala Pani of colonial India came to my mind instantly. The British prison on the island was where many revolutionaries were imprisoned. Suddenly, the name started echoing in my mind repeatedly. The British government had left no stone unturned in torturing the revolutionaries, both physically and mentally. The cruelty was so brutal that even the thought of it made one tremble. But the revolutionaries considered the punishment as a garland of flowers and embraced it for Mother India and our freedom. This is the same place that even today bears testimony to how our lionhearts faced many privations that we cannot even imagine.

The British used the word 'Kala Pani' as a synonym for deportation. The word 'kala' has its origin in the Sanskrit word '*kaal*', which means 'death' or 'death of time' or water or the place of death – a place where once a person goes, they cannot come back.

Veer Savarkar, the valiant fighter of the freedom struggle, wrote, 'In today's world, there are many lands whose geography is available, but history is not available. Andaman-Nicobar is also one of them. But this land has a very old and profound connection with Indians. It must have been named Andaman because of its egg-like shape.'

About Andaman, Marco Polo wrote, 'It is a vast island, whose ruler is no king. The inhabitants of the island are very cruel and kill and eat people who are of a different kind than them.'

Alarmed by such descriptions, people shied away from coming here till the 17th and 18th centuries. Port Blair was named after Lieutenant Archibald Blair, an officer in the English Navy. The name Port Blair has been changed to Sri Vijaya Puram now. These islands were occupied by the Japanese during the Second World War. At that time, Netaji Subhash Chandra Bose went to the islands and named them Shaheed Dweep and Swaraj Dweep, respectively. On 23 January 2023, on the occasion of Netaji Subhash Chandra Bose's 126th Birth Anniversary, 21 islands in the Andaman and Nicobar were named after all the 21st recipients of the highest gallantry award, Param Vir Chakra.

We landed on an Air India flight at Veer Savarkar International Airport, Port Blair, one morning. We had flown in from Chennai. The first stop was, of course, the Cellular Jail. This jail is a silent witness to the cruelty inflicted by the British on Indian freedom fighters. This prison was also called Kala Pani because it was thousands of kilometres away from mainland India. Secondly, it was surrounded by water on all sides, and no prisoner could escape. And even if one tried to escape, he could only jump into the water and die. This prison was built with this frightful intention. Indian revolutionaries were tortured in terrible ways in jail. There is a model of an oil press inside the prison, where prisoners were used in place of oxen to extract oil. Beating the prisoners with whips daily and starving them was a very common practice.

In fact, after the Revolt of 1857, the British Government contemplated that the captured revolutionaries should be sent to a place that was completely isolated from mainland India. So, they sent about 4,000 revolutionaries to the Andaman and Nicobar Islands. First, the Indian revolutionaries were sent to Ross Island, where they were tasked with clearing the forest and preparing residences for British officers. The Indian revolutionaries faced dangers like snakes and scorpions in the treacherous islands. They would spend the entire day cutting wood, and at night, the mosquitoes and other poisonous insects would not let them sleep. Many revolutionaries made the supreme sacrifice as they faced these adversities. Diseases like malaria took many lives as well. Viper Island was also cleared by the British Government for the same purpose.

In 1890, the British Government formed a two-member committee and asked it to submit a report about the captives' colony in Andaman. In their report, they said that the purpose of creating a captives' colony in Andaman was that it should work as an alternative to the death penalty, but the prison of Andaman did not fulfil this condition. Therefore, they suggested that the prisoners should be made to undergo harsh prison sentences in the initial days. For this, they proposed that for the first six months, the prisoners should undergo imprisonment in specially constructed solitary cells in a jail. In this way, the foundation for the Cellular Jail was laid.

The construction of Cellular Jail started in 1896 and was completed in 1906. About 600 prisoners were engaged in its construction, and about 30 lakh bricks were used. With a tower in the middle, which worked as the central point, a three-storey building with 693 cells spread over seven corridors was constructed. The Cellular Jail has been constructed in such a way that all seven blocks meet at one point, which makes monitoring the prisoners easier. The cells were designed in a way that the prisoners would not be able to socialize with or talk to each other. Not only could the prisoners not communicate with each other, but they could not even see each other's faces. It was ironic that while on the one hand, Swami Vivekananda was talking about the free expression of human civilization in Chicago on 11th September 1893, on the other hand, the British Government was making new plans every day to crush the Indians with oppression.

There are two towers at the entrance of the Cellular Jail. On them is written in big letters – 'National Memorial'. It was inaugurated by the then Prime Minister Shri Morarji Desai on 11th February 1979. As soon as one enters, there is a museum on the right where the lives of the brave revolutionaries have been recounted. The first is of Baba Bhansingh, who was brought here in the Lahore Conspiracy Case to serve a harsh life sentence. The prison staff beat him so brutally that he died a martyr in the prison.

Mahavir Singh is next, a member of the Hindustan Socialist Republican Association and a comrade of Sardar Bhagat Singh. He took part in a hunger strike in the jail. To forcefully break the strike, the prison staff forcibly filled his nostrils with milk, and he died. The authorities then tied his body to a stone and tossed it into the sea. When this news reached the mainland, people were outraged at the barbarity of the authorities.

Yet another great revolutionary was Indubhushan Roy. He was sentenced to prison for ten years in the Alipore Manicktolla case. The inhuman and harrowing treatment in jail made him mentally ill. Fed up with the daily torture, he tied his coat to the prison's grill and hanged himself.

As we proceeded, we saw the *Swatantrya Jyoti* or the Eternal Flame of Freedom, blazing continuously, paying tribute to our bravehearts to remind us that their sacrifices will never be forgotten. As we walked a little further, we saw several chairs set up, where a light and sound show takes place every night, describing the jail and the freedom fighters in detail. The gallows on the right, where the nooses are still hung to give an idea of how the prisoners were hanged, were eerie. Whenever someone was hanged, all the prisoners were ordered to watch, to purposely show them the punishment meted out. A bell would be rung, and the lights turned on to remind the prisoners of the consequences of their 'crimes'.

In front of the gallows is the crusher, where mannequins have been installed to show how the prisoners extracted oil. Every prisoner had a certain quota. Some prisoners had to extract oil, while some had to make coconut fibre. It was mandatory to extract thirty pounds of oil every day, and if it was not, the prisoners would be beaten. Even drinking water was given in a limited quantity.

Veer Savarkar has described the hardships in his autobiography '*My Transportation for Life*'. He writes that no matter what the circumstances were, the jail authorities were not bothered. All they cared about was getting their thirty pounds of oil per day. If the oil was not extracted as per the target, the barbaric jailer David Barry would abuse and humiliate the prisoners. They were completely at his mercy. Barry was known to be among the most vicious of the jailers. Who knows how many souls he might have tormented? Perhaps that is why he met such a painful end. He became paralyzed and died before he could return to England.

As I walked through the corridors, I had goosebumps and was filled with immense reverence. I repeatedly saluted the bravehearts in my heart. And why wouldn't I? After all, we all owe a debt to the revolutionaries for the lives we are leading today. It is because of their sacrifices that we can breathe the air of freedom in our motherland. They helped us to break the shackles of colonialism by sacrificing their youth and their lives. We will remain forever in their debt.

As soon as I stepped into Veer Savarkar's cell, I became very emotional. It was surreal that I was standing in the very cell where the brave freedom fighter was tied with chains and made to stand upside down against the wall so that he could not talk to anyone. There is a photograph of Veer Savarkar in the cell with a garland of flowers around it. Savarkar's extraordinary intellect can be gauged from the fact that during his ten years of incarceration, he wrote many poems in honour of Mother India. He would write the lines on the wall with a piece of coal and then memorize them. When he was released from prison, he wrote down all the 6,000 lines, which he had memorized during his stay in prison, in the form of a book. There is a famous quote from him in Sanskrit, which he wrote during his stay in jail.

आसिन्धु-सिन्धु-पर्यन्ता यस्य भारतभूमिका।
पितृभूः पुण्यभूश्चैव स वै हिन्दुरिति स्मृतः॥

(That is, the one who considers this land of India extending from the Indus to the sea as his fatherland, a sacred land, is a Hindu.)

Veer Savarkar's elder brother, Ganesh Damodar Savarkar, was also imprisoned in the same jail. But the workings of fate were such that both the brothers did not even meet for two years. After I visited the Cellular Jail in December 2012, I had the honour of visiting Veer Savarkar's memorial in June 2016. This monument is located right in front of Shivaji Park in Mumbai. Later, I also had the opportunity to visit his birthplace, Bhagur, in Nashik district. It was indeed humbling to see the place where he grew up. I believe it is imperative that every Indian should visit these hallowed places whenever they get an opportunity. We will never be able to repay the debt we owe them for our freedom, but by visiting these places, we can definitely pay our respects.

Another notable name sent to Kala Pani was Batukeshwar Dutt, who, along with Bhagat Singh, had raised the cry for freedom by throwing a bomb in the Central Assembly on 8th April 1929. Batukeshwar Dutt was an active member of the Hindustan Socialist Republican Association.

He was released a few years before Independence. However, a few years later, he became sick with tuberculosis and breathed his last in AIIMS in Delhi in 1965. His last rites were performed as per his wish at Hussainiwala, where three of his old comrades – Bhagat Singh, Rajguru and Sukhdev were cremated. His samadhi is present in Hussainiwala even today.

I have listed down a few of the eminent revolutionaries who were sent to the Cellular Jail:

1. Veer Savarkar and his brother Ganesh Damodar Savarkar
2. Batukeshwar Dutt
3. Jaidev Kapoor
4. Hotilal Verma
5. Baburam Hari
6. Pt. Parmanand
7. Ladha Ram
8. Indu Bhushan Roy
9. Prithvi Singh Azad
10. Deevan Singh
11. Pulin Das
12. Trilokinath Chakravarti
13. Gurmukh Singh
14. Yogendra Shukla
15. Maulana Ahmadullah
16. Nand Gopal Chopra
17. Bhai Parmanand
18. Mohan Singh
19. Upendranath Banerjee
20. Birendra Chand Sen
21. Vishwanath Mathur

Apart from the names in this list, there were thousands who happily sacrificed their lives for Mother India. It may not be possible to mention all of them, but the country can never forget their supreme sacrifice.

By 1937, native governments came to power in different parts of the country. There were continuous hunger strikes in the jail, and the British Government began to crumble. By 1938, the Cellular Jail was vacated. The area was occupied by the Japanese from 1942 to 1945. On 29th December 1943, in the midst of World War II, Subhash Chandra Bose came to the Andamans and paid tribute to the bravehearts and hoisted the tricolour. Subhash Chandra Bose was someone who forcefully talked about the agony of slavery in India and the atrocities of British rule, not only at the national but also at the international level. He had declared, "Give me blood, and I'll give you freedom'. It is what he believed in. The ways of the Moderates were not for him, and he formed the Azad Hind Fauj to overthrow the British.

I decided to visit his house, which is known as Netaji Bhawan and is a museum. It was built in 1909 by Netaji's father Shri Janakinath Bose. This building is situated on Lala Lajpat Rai Marg (Sarani) in Calcutta. In this historical building, Netaji's office, his bedroom, the clothes used by him and many of his old photographs have been preserved, which give us a glimpse of Netaji's rich past. The Azad Hind Fauj uniform that Subhash Babu wore is still intact.

In June 2017, I had the opportunity to go to Tokyo, Japan. There, I had the honour of offering prayers at the Renkō-ji Temple, built by the Japanese in memory of Netaji. It is assumed to be the purported location of the ashes of Netaji, though it is widely believed he perished in a plane crash. It is still controversial. My only aim was to pay my respects to Netaji. I also believe that Netaji did not die in a plane crash. Every year, on 23rd January (his birthday), thousands of Japanese citizens gather here and pay tribute to Netaji.

In 1941, to escape house arrest, Subhash Babu left for Berlin from this very place. At one time, even Mahatma Gandhi and Nehru had come here. In 2007, Shinzo Abe, the then Prime Minister of Japan, also visited this place. We also paid an emotional tribute to Subhash Babu. Colonel Gurbaksh Singh, a famous soldier in Azad Hind Fauj, had composed a song titled 'Netaji Ke Farman'. I consider it necessary to quote for you some of its lines:-

Get up, awaken the fortunes of slumbering India,
This is how we take freedom, take it young and show it.

The Cellular Jail is the most venerable of pilgrimages, and we should never forget its significance. Rather it is our responsibility to continue telling the future generations about the great revolutionaries and keep the flame of patriotism glowing. The place, which till yesterday was the symbol of the cruelty of British rule, is today a national memorial dedicated to the saga of bravery of the Indian Independence movement.

4

The Sons of Punjab

Another chapter in Indian history is the terrible Jallianwala Bagh Massacre. Never did the British Government carry out such a heinous massacre of this magnitude at any point during the Indian Independence Movement. It was a barbaric act, unforgettable as well as unforgivable. Although the British Government inflicted many wounds on the Indians, this was such a deep wound that it continues to hurt us to this very day. No visitor can remain unaffected when he or she sees the bullet marks on the walls, imagining the tragic event that took the lives of so many innocent men, women and children. This great symbol of our freedom struggle is the holiest of pilgrimage sites. One's birth in the blessed land of India is meaningless if one does not visit this place at least once in a lifetime and pay homage to the bravehearts.

Jallianwala Bagh is located very close to Gurdwara Harmandir Sahib, i.e. the Golden Temple in the city of Amritsar, which is one of the largest districts of Punjab. I went there for the first time in 1995. It was an emotional moment for me. Since childhood, I had been hearing and reading the stories of Jallianwala Bagh, of how General Reginald Dyer had opened fire on unarmed Indians. Stories about how a garden had turned into a place besmirched with blood and filled with piles of dead bodies. As I stood there, I wondered what the fault of the innocent people was. I could not understand the depravity of General Dyer's mind. How could one justify the act under any circumstances? The truth is that one cannot.

Before we comprehend the Jallianwala Bagh incident, we need to understand the ongoing political events of the time, which made the British so desperate that they had to resort to such drastic measures. The Sikhs played a major role in the formation of the Ghadar Party in 1913. Lala Hardayal and Sohan Singh Bhakna constantly made efforts to intensify the flames of the freedom struggle in Punjab. They began publishing a newspaper, 'Gadar Di Goonj', in the Punjabi language. However, in 1925, there came a time when fifty revolutionaries of the Ghadar Party were given death sentences, and many others were sent to Kala Pani. Kartar Singh Sarabha, who was the idol of young Bhagat Singh, was hanged at the mere age of nineteen.

Once, Bhagat Singh met Sohan Singh Bhakna, the founder of the Ghadar party, in Amritsar. Bhakna knew that Bhagat Singh's family was quite wealthy and was also aware of Bhagat Singh's zeal. He asked Bhagat Singh,

"Bhagat, you are not lacking in anything. You look good, too. Then why do you want to become a revolutionary at such a young age?"

Bhagat Singh replied, "'You, Ghadar Party and Kartar Singh Sarabha are responsible for this."

On hearing his reply, Sohan Singh asked with wonder, "And how is it so, young man?"

Bhagat Singh replied, "Your love, dedication and willingness to die for the country drove me to become a revolutionary, and now nothing can stop me."

Sohan Singh Bhakna was speechless upon hearing Bhagat Singh's reply and embraced him tightly.

The people of Punjab were enraged because most of the Sikhs from the Ghadar Party had been hanged. Another reason was the introduction of the Rowlatt Act in the country, which allowed the authorities to arrest any person without a trial. However, the British could not cause a rift in Hindu-Sikh-Muslim unity despite trying their best. Overall, the British policy of 'Divide and Rule" did not prove to be effective. Dr Satyapal and Dr Saifuddin Kitchlew fortified Hindu-Muslim communal unity and became an eyesore for the British Government. In April 1919, people of both communities participated enthusiastically in the Ram Navami procession under the leadership of these two leaders. This worried the British a lot. They arrested Dr Saifuddin Kitchlew and Dr Satyapal and quietly sent them out of Amritsar. The news was not disclosed to the general public. This led to widespread anger among the people because both the leaders were much respected by both Hindus and Muslims.

A crowd of about 15,000 people gathered and was on its way to stage a protest outside the deputy commissioner's office. But it was stopped near the bridge, which was close to the railway station. Bullets were fired at them, resulting in the death of twelve people and injuring around thirty. This incident led to a further rise in public fury. A missionary school teacher named Miss Sherwood sent six hundred children home due to this strife. On 11th April, when she was leaving Kucha Khurianwala, some people manhandled her and beat her up. This made the British furious, and they resorted to retaliation.

At that time, Michael O'Dwyer was the Lieutenant Governor of Punjab. It is said that this massacre, along with General Dyer, was his doing. He was determined to teach a lesson to the people of Punjab that would hurt them deeply and that they wouldn't forget. The 13th of April 1919 was the date chosen to carry through this ghastly plan. The Sikh sect was founded on 13th April 1699 by Guru Gobind Singh, the tenth guru of the Sikhs. To commemorate this occasion, Baisakhi, the foremost festival of Punjab, is also celebrated. Dyer could not think of a better way to rub salt into the wounds of the people of Punjab. The army conducted a flag march in the city of Amritsar. They were aware that there would be a large gathering in Jallianwala Bagh on that day to hold a peaceful meeting. The meeting started at about 4:30 p.m., and about an hour later, Dyer arrived there with his men. Fortunately, the main entrance of Jallianwala Bagh was narrow, so the tank could not pass through it. In fact, Dyer had come prepared for that, too. At Dyer's orders, ninety Gurkha soldiers and twenty-five Baluch soldiers, with their .303 Lee-Enfield rifles, began firing at unarmed people, including men, women and small children.

This was unexpected and led to mayhem as the crowd began to run for their lives. It led to a stampede in the enclosed garden. It is said that Dyer and his soldiers fired continuously for ten minutes; they fired a total of 1,650 rounds. A total of 388 people were killed, and 200 people were injured in that firing. However, according to unofficial figures, more than a thousand people were killed, and more than two thousand were injured.

It was a terrifying scenario. Many perished in the stampede. Some jumped into the well there to save themselves. Later, more than a hundred bodies were recovered from the well. Even today, the bullet marks on the walls of Jallianwala Bagh carry the memories of the haunting incident. This massacre had a very deep impact. It was unprecedented, and there was no justification. It shook the Indians to the core, not only within the country but also abroad.

The next day, little Bhagat Singh, who was then only an eleven-year-old boy, went from Lahore to Jallianwala Bagh and brought back some of the blood-soaked soil. Even at that young age, the incident had shaken him to the core and would deeply influence his life. This incident had a huge impact on millions of Indians. Sardar Udham Singh was one of them. He was extremely anguished. Udham Singh had been present during this heinous carnage. He and one of his friends had been arranging water for the people. Udham Singh's father worked as a railway gatekeeper. Singh was born on 26th December 1899 in the Sangrur district of Punjab. His parents died in his childhood. He was brought up in an orphanage in Putlighar, Amritsar.

He was an eyewitness to the massacre, and he could never forget it. He pledged to kill Michael O'Dwyer to exact revenge. And he made it the purpose of his life. After the Jallianwala massacre, he left the orphanage and started working for the country alongside the revolutionaries. Udham Singh was a big supporter of communal unity and changed his name to Ram Mohammad Singh Azad to symbolize this unity.

In 1924, he travelled to the US and came in contact with the Ghadar Party. Acting on the advice of Bhagat Singh, he returned to India with twenty-five revolutionaries and many weapons so that the revolution could gain momentum. But the British Government got wind of it, and he was arrested under the Arms Act. He was released from jail after a few years. He managed to make his way to London in 1934 to fulfil his goal. He focused on his purpose day and night. He had only one objective – to put Michael O'Dwyer, the former Lieutenant Governor of Punjab, to death. The man responsible for the killings. To accomplish this task, he bought a pistol and six cartridges and then waited for the right moment. Finally, twenty-one years after the Jallianwala Bagh massacre, that day arrived. On 13th March 1940, as Michael O'Dwyer arrived at Caxton Hall of the Royal Central Asian Society in London, Udham Singh took out his pistol (which he had hidden inside a thick book by tearing it) and fired two bullets straight into O'Dwyer's chest, and thus avenged the killing of thousands of innocent Indians. During my visit to London, I had the honour of visiting Caxton Hall. It was surreal to see the place where Jallianwala Bagh massacre was avenged. By killing a British officer on British soil, he proved that the Indian revolutionaries did not lack in spirit. The British Government was shaken. Eventually, on 31st July 1940, he was hanged in London jail. In his memory, a district in Uttarakhand has been named Udham Singh Nagar. Through the efforts of the then Punjab Assembly member Sandhu Singh, the ashes of Udham Singh were brought to India from London, and his last rites were performed at Sangrur, his birthplace.

After travelling through all the states and territories in India, I believe that there is no other city like Amritsar. The cultural heritage, art, attire and food are unrivalled. Before 1947, two cities in Punjab were at the forefront: Lahore and Amritsar. It was because of these cultural and political legacies that the Muslim League wanted to merge Amritsar with Pakistan, whereas the Congress wanted to merge Lahore with India. Both these magnificent cities are situated close to each other. Lahore is only fifty kilometres away from Amritsar. The city of Lahore was inhabited not only by Hindus and Punjabis but also by Bengalis and Tamilians. Lala Lajpat Rai's National College was in Lahore. Bhagat Singh underwent his education in Lahore. At that time, Lahore was the country's cultural capital. Even today, the play *'Jis Lahore nahi dekhya o jamyai nai'* (The One who has not seen the city of Lahore, is not even born) is very famous and is often staged. It was written by Asghar Wajahat. These two cities underwent as much suffering during the Partition as the love and warmth between them at one time. When trains filled with dead bodies of Hindus reached Amritsar from Pakistan, the atmosphere was filled with dread. Similarly, when trains filled with dead bodies of Muslims reached Lahore, the hearts of the people on both sides were filled with bitterness. That bitterness exists even today.

Bhagat Singh, Rajguru and Sukhdev were executed in Lahore jail. Lahore, once the pride of undivided India, was merged with Pakistan.

Well, Amritsar always belonged to us. My first opportunity to visit Amritsar came in January 1995. I had to go there for some inspection work of the railways. I entered the parcel office there and immediately asked where Putlighar was. It was the town where my friend Vivek Mahajan lived. The officer said that he would call Vivek straightaway. I was surprised to see Vivek in front of me within the next five minutes. Since then, I have visited Amritsar at least ten times, and there has never been a single visit when I have not met Vivek. Our relationship has retained the same warmth after all these years.

Amritsar was once a part of Tung village. Guru Ramdas, who was the fourth guru of the Sikhs, bought it from the owners of Tung in 1574 for Rs 700 and founded Amritsar. Amritsar is named after 'Santokhsar Sarovar' which was constructed by Guru Ramdas. Amritsar was built in the form of a walled city like Shahjahanabad in Delhi.

Inside it, there were many *katras*, i.e., colonies built based on castes. Amritsar also has a connection with the Ramayana period. There is the Shri Ram Teerth Temple and the ancient ashram of Rishi Valmiki in Amritsar. According to legend, when Sita left Ayodhya after the *agni pariksha*, Sage Valmiki gave her shelter in this ashram. There are many temples in this temple complex dating back to the period, including an old pond on its premises. Lord Ram's sons, Luv and Kush, were born in this ashram. Inside the complex are Sage Valmiki's hut and the step-well in which Sita used to bathe. Both the structures have been preserved.

The world-renowned Grand Trunk Road, built by Sher Shah Suri, passes through Amritsar. Once upon a time, the Grand Trunk Road started from Peshawar and went to Bangladesh. Today, Amritsar is mainly known for the Golden Temple, which is the largest gurudwara, and the *langar* here is famous all over the world. It is the holy pilgrimage site of the Sikhs, where scores of people from various communities from all over the world come to pay obeisance. It is also called Harmandir Sahib or the Temple of Hari. The foundation of Harmandir Sahib was laid in December 1588 by Hazrat Mian Mirji, a Sufi saint from Lahore, at the initiative of Guru Arjun Dev, the fifth guru of the Sikhs. The gurudwara was completed in the year 1604. The *langar* here is famous all over the world. Approximately 50,000 devotees partake in langar every day at the temple. On weekends and during festivals, the number of people partaking in langar reaches one lakh. Langar is served twenty-four hours a day to all the devotees visiting the Golden Temple. This practice was started by Sri Guru Nanak Dev, the first guru of Sikhs, and it was made a perpetual tradition by Sri Guru Amar Das, the third guru of the Sikhs.

There are two langar halls in the Golden Temple, where langar is served to the devotees. In these halls, a total of 5,000 people can eat at the same time. In this langar, about 50 quintals of flour, 18 quintals of pulses, 14 quintals of rice, and seven quintals of milk are consumed every day. Along with this, 100 gas cylinders are also required every day to cook. There is also a roti-making machine, which can make about 25,000 rotis in an hour. Special attention is paid to cleanliness and hygiene in the langar halls. After people finish their meal, the used plates and utensils are washed in five stages before they are used again. All the devotees are seated together on mats in rows without any discrimination based on race, caste, colour or status. Devotees come from all over the country and abroad and offer services at the Golden Temple in whichever way they can, and in return to gain immense happiness.

Harmandir Sahib suffered a lot of damage during the Afghan attack in the 19th century. Maharaja Ranjit Singh had it rebuilt and plated with gold. Since then, it has been called the Golden Temple. The plan for this 400-year-old gurdwara was prepared by Guru Arjun Dev himself.

The temple has four entry gates, which open in four directions. At that time, the society was divided into four castes. These four gates welcome people of every caste, and there is no discrimination. There is an ancient Beri tree called Dukh Bhanjani in the yard of Harmandir Sahib. It is believed that the person who gets the *beris* of this tree has fulfilled every wish and is liberated from all his sorrows. Dukh Bhanjani, the beri that breaks (ends) sorrows. Even now, it is believed that God puts an end to all the sorrows and fulfils all good desires of the person who bathes in the Amritsar Lake, which is beneath this Dukh Bhanjani Beri.

Madan Lal Dhingra is another name associated with this city. He was born on 18th September, 1883 in an affluent family in Amritsar. In the early days of the revolution, he killed Curzon Wyllie in London, which caused a sensation across the country.

His father was a civil surgeon in Amritsar. He sent Madan Lal to London for higher education. In London, Madan Lal came in contact with great revolutionaries like Veer Savarkar and Shyamji Krishna Varma.

Savarkar made Madan Lal Dhingra a member of the revolutionary organization called Abhinav Bharat and trained him in the use of weapons. At that time, Dhingra lived in India House in London, which was the main hub of the revolutionaries.

As Indian revolutionaries were being executed one after the other, there was extreme anger among all of them. On 1st July 1909, when Curzon Wyllie arrived to attend the Indian National Association programme, Madan Lal Dhingra fired five bullets into his face. He was arrested, and eventually, Madan Lal Dhingra was hanged on 17th August 1909 in Pentonville Prison. He died a martyr, even though his family did not approve of his revolutionary activities. His father had even given an advertisement in the newspaper declaring that he and his family had severed ties with him. But he is hailed as a martyr, and in Amritsar, his

At **Ganesh Wada,**
birthplace of Rani Laxmi Bai.

At **Barrackpore,** the site of
Mangal Pandey's execution.

At Chandra Shekhar Azad's
birthplace in **Madhya Pradesh.**

At the Gadar Memorial in
San Francisco, USA.

At **Jallianwala Bagh** where the bullet marks are still present.

At Bhagat Singh's ancestral house at **Khatkar Kalan.**

With Yadvinder Singh, grandson of
Shaheed-e-Azam Bhagat Singh's younger brother.

At the birth place of Veer Savarkar,
Bhagur, Nasik.

The Cellular Jail at
Sri Vijaya Puram (Port Blair).

At the India House,
London.

At CQMH Abdul Hamid,
PVC's, Mazaar.

At Renkoji Temple in **Tokyo.**
It is said that ashes of
Netaji Subhas Chandra Bose are lying here.

With Brig Kuldeep Singh Chandpuri,
MVC, VSM.

At **Longewala** Post.

At the Samadhi Sthal of Tatya Tope, in **Shivpuri, Madhya Pradesh.**

At the **Kargil War Memorial.**

LOC at Kargil.

At **Leh** War Memorial.

At **Rezang La** War Memorial.

At the **Siachen** War Memorial.

Jaswantgarh War Memorial.

At **Palam,** Indian Air Force Museum
with the statue of Flying Officer Nirmal Jit Singh Sekhon, PVC.

With Maj Gen **Ian Cardozo,**
AVSM, SM.

With Sub Maj (Hon Capt)
Bana Singh, PVC.

With Capt (Hon Maj) **Hari Pal Singh Ahluwalia.**

With **Meena Nayyar**, the mother of Capt Anuj Nayyar, MVC.

With Sub Maj (Hon Capt) **Yogendra Singh Yadav**, PVC.

With Sub Maj **Sanjay Kumar**, PVC.

At Palampur, with Girdhari Lal Batra
and Kamal Kanta Batra,
parents of Capt Vikram Batra, PVC.

With Mohini Pandey,
mother of Capt Manoj Kumar Pandey,
PVC and his brother Manmohan
at their residence in Lucknow.

With Nutan Batra Malik,
sister of Capt Vikram Batra, PVC.

With Dr NK Kalia and Vijaya Kalia,
the parents of Capt Saurabh Kalia.

With Col VN Thapar,
the father of
Capt Vijayant Thapar, VrC.

life-size statue was installed at the centre of the city, and the bus stand there was named after him.

The Pakistan border is only twenty-eight kilometres away from Amritsar. The point from where one enters the Lahore district of Pakistan is known as the Attari border. After the 1971 war, when the Ferozepur border was closed for trade, Attari became the centre of all business and political activities. Even today, many commercial vehicles enter from this point. In 1999, the then Prime Minister Atal Bihari Vajpayee's 'Aman ki Asha' bus also entered Pakistan from this point. It is also the bus route that used to run between Delhi and Lahore.

A grand flag-lowering ceremony takes place every evening at the Attari border, for which a large number of people from both countries gather. Compared to Ferozepur, the ceremony is quite grand. There is tremendous enthusiasm among the people, and patriotism is at its peak. The atmosphere echoes with the deafening slogans of '*Bharat Mata ki Jai*' and '*Vande Mataram*'. Just before the Attari border is the last railway station in India – Attari. This is the last station for the movement of trains between India and Pakistan.

Many great personalities were born in Amritsar. Among them are the great revolutionary Madan Lal Dhingra, famous singer Mohammad Rafi, first woman IPS officer Kiran Bedi, cricketer Navjyot Singh Sidhu, bhajan singer Narendra Chanchal, and India's first Field Marshal Sam Manekshaw.

The historical, cultural and political significance of Amritsar makes it a city one must surely visit. The ancient city has been the birthplace of bravehearts who have laid down their lives for the country and has been a witness to events that have altered the history of the nation.

5

Siachen: The Men at the Frontier

Sleep peacefully at your homes, the Indian Army is guarding the frontiers.

It was the month of July 2023. I was having tea at the residence of Lt Col Shashikant Sharma in Barrackpore. As we chatted, he told me that he had been posted in Siachen twice. When I heard this, I was excited and immediately asked him, "Sharmaji, I have wanted to visit the Siachen area for many years. Can I go there?"

He immediately replied, "You can certainly go there. However, you can only go up to the Siachen Base Camp because the route beyond the base camp is extremely inaccessible, and one has to undergo special training at the base camp before travelling on that route. And yes, it is mandatory to obtain permission from the Indian Army for this."

Upon hearing this, I felt that my dream would be fulfilled soon. However, I did not expect that God would answer my prayer rather quickly. Exactly two months after I returned from Barrackpore, I got a chance to travel to Siachen Base Camp. Siachen was first mentioned in a report in 1848 by a British citizen named Henry Strachey. When I reached the Siachen Base Camp, I could not believe that I was really there. But indeed, my dream had turned into reality. On 25th September 2016, we took a flight from Delhi and landed in Leh at 7 a.m. After resting the entire day to acclimatize our bodies to the weather and altitude, our first stop was the war memorial in Leh to pay homage to the bravehearts. In the museum named Hall of Fame, information about the wars fought in Leh and Kargil regions has been given, and various types of weapons won from the enemies are also on display. Detailed information about the heroic stories and bravery of the Param Vir Chakra and Mahavir Chakra winners can also be found.

The Hall of Fame was established in 1986, and its extension opened to the public in June 2016. This place consists of three wings – War Memorial, War Museum and Shaurya Sthal (a memorial with the names of bravehearts on it). Recently, the Hall of Fame was chosen as the best museum in India and features among the best twenty-five museums in Asia.

Every evening, an army troop conducts a flag-lowering ceremony while saluting the bravehearts. The next day, with the first rays of the sun, the national flag is again hoisted with honour. This ceremony lasts for about fifteen minutes. After that, a documentary made on the Kargil War is shown in the yard of this war memorial; every Indian's eyes become moist after watching this film. This film shows how our soldiers gave a befitting reply to the enemy and won the war.

Just a week before I visited Leh, Pakistani terrorists had carried out a cowardly attack on the Uri military camp. Eighteen soldiers who were asleep at the time were killed in the attack. As a result, the atmosphere on the international border was tense. As per the schedule, we were to leave for Siachen Base Camp the next morning. But we were concerned as we had not received permission yet. Over dinner, we decided that if we did not get permission from the army, we would stay back in Nubra Valley. The next morning, albeit a little late, we received permission. We were thrilled and immediately set off.

Driving along one of the world's highest motorable roads at Khardung La Pass, which is at an altitude of 18,380 feet, we reached the army's first TCP (Traffic Control Post) at Sasoma via Nubra Valley at 5 p.m. On the way, we saw the beautiful view of the Shyok River. It is a forty-kilometre journey from Sasoma to the base camp, and the road winds along the banks of the Nubra River, which originates from Siachen Glacier. A little further, the Nubra and Shyok rivers merge and then join the Sindhu River in Baltistan. To the west of Siachen is the Saltoro mountain range, which divides Baltistan and the Nubra Valley of Ladakh. In the Balti language, 'Siachen' means 'a place where roses are in abundance'.

It was close to seven in the evening when we finally arrived at our destination. We first went to the Siachen War Memorial and paid homage to the bravehearts. In December 2015, the Defence Minister told the Parliament that since 1984, 869 soldiers had made the supreme sacrifice in Siachen. Unfortunately, most of these soldiers made the supreme sacrifice due to the harsh weather. In February 2016, we lost ten of our soldiers in a snowstorm. It speaks of the difficult conditions in which our soldiers stay. The weather is brutal, and in the winters, the cold is unimaginable. Yet they stoically defend the borders of our nation.

At the Siachen Memorial, a helmet is hung over an upside-down gun, reminding us of the sacrifice of the bravehearts. The Siachen Base Camp is at an altitude of 13,000 feet, while the altitude of the posts built on the glacier goes up to 21,000 feet. There are about 160 posts of the Indian Army here. At these posts, officers are deployed along with soldiers. Pakistan is only at a distance of thirteen kilometres from Siachen Base Camp. That is why we have deployed our artillery, on the banks of the Nubra River at the base camp. This interesting piece of information was given to us by the base commander appointed at the base camp.

Now let me introduce you to the history and geography of Siachen. The snow-clad Siachen Glacier arises from the mighty Karakoram mountain range. The length of this glacier is 76.4 km. The temperature here ranges from zero to -70 degrees. Due to its temperature, Siachen is also called the Third Pole as the climate is akin to the two poles, giving one an idea of the sub-zero temperatures our soldiers have to work in.

The landscape is awe-inspiring as it is treacherous. All the soldiers and officers have to reach their posts on foot. Helicopters deliver food and supplies from the base camp to the posts built in the snow-clad area above. Before being posted, every soldier has to undergo five weeks of rigorous training at the Siachen Base Camp. Then they are sent to Siachen Glacier on a three-month appointment. The Siachen Battle School of the Army provides this training. Apart from this, the teams climbing Everest are also trained here. For the last few years, the Army has been inviting commoners and giving them the opportunity to trek the glacier. For this, entries are invited through advertisements, and members are selected based on their physical ability and experience. The Northern Command of the Army executes the entire programme. This is a commendable step and allows the citizens to learn about the difficult circumstances our soldiers are engaged in, day and night, to protect us and the country. Sometimes, it takes them as long as twenty-one days just to reach their posts!

By the time our meeting with the base commander was over, it was quite dark. From there, we had to go to a place called Sumur, which was about eighty kilometres from the base camp. The colonel warned us to be careful because the water level of the Nubra river has the tendency to suddenly rise, and as the base camp is situated on the banks of the Nubra River, they are always on alert. There is an iron bridge across the river one has to cross to reach the base camp. There is a well-known saying among the people of this region – 'This place is so barren, and its valleys are so high that only the strongest friends and staunchest enemies come here.' Spending every single moment here is a challenge. Surviving on the highest battlefield in the world is very tough, but our soldiers do it effortlessly. Their devotion and passion towards the country give them strength and motivation every moment to face every adversity.

Ice is melted and chlorine tablets are added to it to make the water safe to drink. During deployment here, one often cannot sleep, memory declines, weight starts decreasing, and AMC (Acute Mountain Sickness) is common. Despite such adverse conditions, every army soldier and officer dreams of getting deployed at Siachen at least once, although they are well aware of the challenges. Salute to this spirit and bravery!

After the Kashmir War of 1947-48, India and Pakistan reached an agreement in 1949 on the border, defining the Ceasefire Line. But there was an omission here. In this agreement, the last point just before Siachen Glacier was marked as NJ 9842, and the part beyond Siachen Glacier was not demarcated. Further, it was written that 'and after this in the north of the glaciers', which became a point of dispute. In the Shimla Agreement of 1972, the Ceasefire Line was declared as the Line of Control. In the LOC Shimla Agreement, we had a golden opportunity to highlight the sentence 'and after this in the north of the glaciers'. However, we could not seize that opportunity because it is said that Bhutto convinced Indira Gandhi to implement it later, but that opportunity never arose again.

In 1980, Pakistan increased its movement in this area under the pretext of mountaineering. In 1982-83, it became evident that Pakistan's intentions regarding this region were suspicious. By 1984, Pakistan had constructed several outposts on the Saltoro mountain range occupying the area. There were reports that by 17th April 1984, Pakistan could capture other areas, too. As soon as this became known, the Indian Army sprang into action. With the Indian Air Force in the lead, India started Operation Meghdoot and chased away Pakistani soldiers from this area. The army first captured Bilafond La and Sia La. The Cheetah helicopter played a crucial role in this operation. At that time, it was the only helicopter that could fly at an altitude of 18,000 feet. On 14th April 1984, India drove the Pakistani soldiers out of the Saltoro mountain range and built posts at such locations from where Pakistan could not even peek at Siachen. In 1987, Pakistan built a post at the highest point and designated it as Quaid Post (named after the founding father of Pakistan, Quaid-e-Azam Muhammad Ali Jinnah). To get rid of Pakistan's presence there, Indian Army launched Operation Rajiv and successfully captured it. Throughout this operation, Subedar Bana Singh displayed unprecedented bravery and made the enemy bite the dust. He was awarded the Param Vir Chakra for this gallantry. The same peak has also been named after him; it is called 'Bana Top'.

From 1984 onwards, India started deploying the Army in this snow-clad area. According to an estimate, deployment of the soldiers in Siachen costs us six crore per day. Sometimes, it also becomes a topic of debate whether this expenditure is justified. In my view, this expenditure is unequivocally justified because Pakistan cannot be trusted under any circumstances. Another reason is that China's border is not very far from here. The strategic area near Baltistan is under the control of China. Considering the growing bonhomie between Pakistan and China, it would be unwise to leave this area unattended. We should not forget that the major reason for the Kargil War was the siege of Siachen.

It is said that Pervez Musharraf, who was the architect of the 1999 Kargil War, was posted in the Siachen region in the 1980s. Musharraf was stunned when India threw the Pakistani soldiers out of Siachen. Triggered by this incident, he made a plan for the Kargil War. Once a journalist asked Musharraf why Pakistan started the Kargil War. Musharraf retorted, "Why did India start Siachen?"

His response answered many unspoken questions. Several rounds of Siachen peace talks have taken place to date. The last talks were held on 23rd November 2003, in which both sides decided to fully implement the ceasefire and the situation has been peaceful since then.

There is a temple of OP Baba (Om Prakash Baba) in the base camp area, where every soldier offers prayers and seeks blessings from him before leaving for the glacier. OP Baba was employed in the army, and it is said that his soul resides here even today and that he protects the soldiers from every calamity. This is the third temple in the army area that we learned about. On the way to Tawang, a temple dedicated to Jaswant Singh ji was built at Jaswant Garh Memorial, while a temple dedicated to Harbhajan Baba was built at Nathu La in Sikkim. It is believed that the spirits of ex-soldiers in these three temples still protect and guard the soldiers from impending danger.

Among the leaders of the nation who visited Siachen the most number of times, the name of the then Defence Minister George Fernandes is at the top. He tried to solve every problem faced by the soldiers with great sincerity and was successful in doing so. He would frown at the delay in purchasing the items needed by the Army. As a swift solution to this problem, he ordered the Defence Secretary to visit Siachen so that he would understand the conditions under which our soldiers perform their duties. As a result, all the equipment was soon made available.

In June 2005, Manmohan Singh became the first Prime Minister of India to visit Siachen, and Dr APJ Abdul Kalam became the first President of India to visit the border. Narendra Modi visited Siachen when he became the prime minister and encouraged and praised the soldiers.

After having a cup of steaming hot tea and discussing various topics, we took leave of the base commander. We again paid homage to the bravehearts and left Siachen Base Camp for our next destination. It was indeed a memorable visit from the awe-inspiring mountains and landscape and the treacherous journey, to getting an idea of how the Army protects its borders selflessly in the harshest of conditions. The freedom we enjoy comes at a price and we must never take it for granted.

6

Kashmir and the India-Pak War of 1947-48: Protectors of Paradise

Gar firdaus bar rue zami ast, hami asto, hami asto, hami ast.
(If there is heaven anywhere on earth, it is here, it is here, it is here)

—Amir Khusro

As we all know, India became independent on 15th August 1947. But before that, the country was made up of 565 princely states, and all of them were given the freedom of choice to merge with either India or Pakistan. Sardar Patel accomplished this challenging task. Except for Junagadh and Hyderabad, all the other princely states accepted the Instrument of Accession and joined India. Furthermore, the state of Goa joined India in 1961. However, the merger of Kashmir was still pending. Being a Kashmiri, Nehru had a soft spot for Kashmir. So, he took upon himself the task of merging Kashmir.

Jammu and Kashmir was ruled by the Dogra kings for 200 years. Jammu and Kashmir is the only state in India where Hindu kings governed the Hindu majority for 200 years, but now, sadly, the situation is such that the Hindu Kashmiri Pandits have been living in exile for years. Coming back to 1947, the then-ruler Maharaja Hari Singh refused to accede to either India or Pakistan. But Pakistan had evil intentions of seizing Kashmir right from the beginning. Jinnah believed that no one could stop Kashmir from merging with Pakistan. With these nefarious intentions, he sent tribal infiltrators to Kashmir to occupy it forcibly. On 20th October 1947, Pakistan gave arms to the Pathans in Abbottabad and also sent its soldiers disguised as Pathans with them to attack Kashmir.

The tribals moved via Abbottabad-Muzaffarabad-Uri-Poonch and directly entered Baramulla to begin their attack. It was the 22nd of October. They caused a maelstrom of brutality. They not only committed arson, vandalism and murders but also raped women. Maharaja Hari Singh of Jammu and Kashmir understood the vile intentions of Pakistan and signed the Instrument of Accession with India on 26th October 1947. The then Governor General Lord Mountbatten validated the Instrument of Accession, and it immediately came into effect on 27th October 1947. With its implementation, the Indian Army entered Kashmir on the very same day.

Pandit Nehru had special orders that before landing at the Srinagar airstrip, there should be no Pakistani aircraft there. So, when Air Force pilot Biju Patnaik flew down Lieutenant Colonel Ranjit Rai and his seventeen soldiers, he first circled the Srinagar airfield twice and ensured that no Pakistani aircraft would attack them.

After this, Lt Col Ranjit Rai got down to his job and began making all efforts to save Baramulla from the clutches of the enemy. Before long, the Pathans once again launched a lethal attack, and in that attack, Lt Col Ranjit Rai made the supreme sacrifice. He was the first officer of the Indian Army to lay down his life for Kashmir.

On 2nd November, Brigadier Lionel Protip Sen was sent to the Kashmir Valley. He displayed unprecedented bravery and battered the enemy. The Indian Army managed to save the Srinagar airport from falling into the hands of Pakistan. After this, campaigns to completely drive them out of the valley continued for several months. Ultimately, in August 1948, the United Nations adopted a ceasefire resolution. During this period, there were many attacks on Kashmir, and many people were killed. But in the end, India won. As a result of the ceasefire, everything remained as it was. This essentially means that Pakistan occupies nearly 34 per cent of the area of Jammu and Kashmir, which is today called as Pakistan-Occupied Kashmir. It is an integral part of India, though, under the agreement made with Maharaja Hari Singh of Jammu and Kashmir and remains a bone of contention between the two countries.

While discussing this war, it is necessary to mention a courageous man who, at the time of partition, was said to have been invited by Jinnah for the post of the Army Chief of Pakistan for his bravery. But he rejected the offer straightaway. The name of that hero was Brigadier Mohammad Usman.

When he declined the offer, Jinnah was annoyed and announced a reward of Rs 50,000 for anyone who would behead him. It had hurt his ego. You can imagine the value of such a huge amount of money in 1947. Brig Mohammad Usman was born on 15th July 1912 in the Mau district of Uttar Pradesh. He lay down his life on 3rd July 1948 in the war on the soil of Kashmir. He was killed in action while capturing the Naushera area. He is the only brigadier in the history of the Indian Army who sacrificed his life on the battlefield. Generally, high-ranking officers do not go to the front to fight. He not only went to the frontlines, but he also fought shoulder-to-shoulder with his men and slept on the ground with them. For his gallantry, he is known as the 'Lion of Naushera'. He was buried in Jamia Millia Islamia, Delhi, and the then-prime minister, Pandit Nehru, attended his funeral. I also had a chance to go to his grave and pay my respects.

It is impossible to talk about the war of 1947 without mentioning Major Somnath Sharma. Despite breaking his arm while playing hockey, he saved the Budgam area from the attack of the tribals while making the supreme sacrifice. Shortly before a martyr's death, Maj Somnath Sharma, in his message to the headquarters, said, "The enemy is only fifty yards away from us. But we will not retreat even an inch." With his men, he repulsed more than 500 enemy forces, causing heavy casualties, till he himself died fighting till his last breath. He was only twenty-four years of age.

Apart from Maj Sharma, Company Havildar Major Piru Singh Shekhawat, Lance Naik Karam Singh, Naik Jadunath Singh, and Second Lieutenant Ram Raghoba Rane played a decisive role in the battle of Kashmir. Maj Sharma was the first recipient of the Param Vir Chakra in the history of independent India. The Param Vir Chakra was instituted on 26th January 1950, the highest military decoration. It was only because of him and his brave comrades that the Srinagar airbase wasn't captured by the enemy. As a tribute to him, his statue is mounted near the entrance of the Srinagar airport.

The Zoji La Pass holds a special place in the battle of the Indian Army against the Pakistani tribals in 1947. For the first time in this battle, the Indian Army used tanks at such a height, a feat that hasn't taken place in the world to date.

In July 1999, while crossing Zoji La Pass, I saw that there was snow in some places. My dream seemed to be coming true. In 1948, when the Pakistanis refused to move from here, General Cariappa made a plan. As per this plan, the tanks were first dismantled, loaded on trucks, and taken to Sonmarg. They were reassembled in Baltal, and then an attack was launched on the enemy. Brigadier Hiralal Atal executed Gen Cariappa's plan, and the codename Operation Bison was given. The enemy could not have imagined such an operation even in their dreams. The tanks launched precise attacks on the enemy and forced Pakistan to flee important areas like Zoji La, Drass and Kargil. Tanks had never been used at such heights anywhere in the world. To keep the movements of the tanks secret, tarpaulins were placed on the trucks, and a curfew was imposed in the areas where the convoy passed so that the enemy would not get even a whiff of it. It was conducted successfully, taking the enemy by utter surprise. Zoji La, Drass and Kargil district in Ladakh were recaptured by the Indian Army. On the 1st of January 1949, a United Nations-mediated ceasefire brought the war to an end.

The valley of Kashmir is drenched in the blood of Brig Mohammad Usman, Maj Somnath Sharma and Lt Ranjit Rai, among countless others. It was the first war fought between two newly independent nations. There were about 6,000 Indian casualties in this battle of Kashmir. Out of them, 1,500 made the supreme sacrifice, 3,500 were injured, and about 1,000 went missing. The five Param Vir Chakras, fifty-three Maha Vir Chakras and more than three hundred Vir Chakras awarded were testimony to the heroism displayed on the battlefield.

7

The India-China War of 1962: Heroes against all Odds

Ae mere watan ke logon, zara ankh mein bhar lo pani,
Jo shaheed hue hain unki, jra yaad karo kurbani.

—Kavi Pradeep

The Sino-Indian War, or the 1962 War, was a military conflict between China and India that took place from 20th October to 21st November. Chushul in Ladakh was at the centre of the 1962 war. While Leh lies at an altitude of 10,000 feet above sea level, Chushul is at approximately 14,231 feet above sea level. At many places, the altitude is up to 15,000 to 17,000 feet. The responsibility of defending a part of this challenging terrain was entrusted to Major Dhan Singh Thapa, 1st Battalion of the 8th Gorkha Rifles. China had been building roads and posts in this area for many years, and unfortunately, our leaders trusted China blindly, which led to the inevitable. The Chinese attacked the Srijap 1 post on 20th October 1962. Maj Thapa and his fellow soldiers gave a befitting reply to the Chinese, though they were less than forty men stationed at the post. Looking at the strength and preparedness of the Chinese Army, it was clear that they would not be able to defeat a large number of Chinese soldiers, but Maj Dhan Singh Thapa did not lose courage and stood his ground till the end. The Chinese soldiers captured him as a prisoner of war, but he did not betray his motherland.

Ultimately, he was released. Maj Dhan Singh Thapa was awarded the Param Vir Chakra for his bravery.

Major Shaitan Singh was given the responsibility of defending the other part of Chushul. The famous lake Pangong Tso also falls in this area. Rezang La is situated a little away from Chushul at an altitude of 18,000 feet. From a strategic point of view, this was an equally significant post like Chushul. Maj Shaitan Singh was leading the troops there. Maj Singh was a Bhati Rajput from Jodhpur, Rajasthan, who was deployed in the 13th Battalion of the Kumaon Regiment. It was on the morning of 18th November that the Chinese attacked his post. Maj Shaitan Singh and his brave comrades gave a befitting reply to the Chinese. He moved through the post, boosting the morale of his men, but was seriously injured in the firing. He had been shot in the stomach and arm, but he continued to motivate his soldiers till he succumbed to his injuries. His body was hidden so that the Chinese couldn't take it away. And three months later, it was recovered under the melting snow with the gun still in his hand. It was sent to his ancestral home with full military honours. Maj Shaitan Singh was posthumously awarded the Param Vir Chakra. Along with him, Naik Hukumchand, Naik Gulab Singh Yadav, Lance Naik Ram Singh, Subedar Ram Kumar and Subedar Ramchander were awarded the Vir Chakra. The Battle of Rezang La is quite exceptional in the history of India. Of the 124 Indian soldiers stationed here, 114 made the supreme sacrifice. But with their bravery and valour, they killed 1,310 Chinese soldiers.

In September 2016, after paying homage to the bravehearts at the Siachen Base Camp, we travelled along the banks of Pangong Tso Lake and reached Chushul. We took a shortcut to go to Chushul, though it is only a dirt track in the name of a road. It took us three hours to cover the distance of forty-five kilometres. On the way, we saw the border posts of ITBP (Indo-Tibetan Border Police). On the banks of Pangong Tso, I had an opportunity to interact with ITBP soldiers. During our interaction, Rajesh Yadav, an inspector in ITBP, described this area to us in detail. He also mentioned that before the 1962 war, Pangong Tso Lake belonged to India. Now, only thirty per cent of it lies in India, while the rest has been seized by China. On our way to Chushul, we saw the post where Maj Dhan Singh Thapa was deployed during the 1962 war. This post is named after him now. The depth of Pangong Tso Lake has not been measured to date. When we tasted the lake water, we realized that its water was not only ice-cold but also salty. The lake is breathtakingly beautiful and almost seems ethereal, merging with the blue sky.

Both the Indian Army and ITBP have many state-of-the-art motorboats in the Pangong area. Among these are state-of-the-art bulletproof motorboats imported from America, which are no less than a wonder. They are very effective in dealing with the enemy in any situation that may arise.

It was dark by the time we reached the ITBP guest house in Chushul. The temperature suddenly started dipping. The soldier in the mess brought us hot momos and tea, which re-energized us. After that, Assistant Commandant Rakesh Kumar showed us the Chinese border and told us in detail about Chushul and Rezang La. He said that in the 1962 war, China suffered its heaviest losses in the Chushul area, and it was here that Maj Shaitan Singh put up a dauntless fight against the Chinese. The stories about Maj Shaitan Singh's valour are very well-known. He knew he did not have adequate weapons and thus would not be able to fight the Chinese soldiers for long. If he wished, he could have retreated since he had also received orders from senior officials to do the same. But he decided to face the enemy like a true soldier. He also gave his fellow soldiers the option to return. But his fellow soldiers were equally brave and decided to stand by their leader.

There was a significant drop in the temperature in Chushul at night. Due to extreme cold, I could not sleep properly. The temperature had dropped to zero on the night of 28th September 2016. It was hard to imagine the weather conditions when Shaitan Singh and his fellow soldiers fought at night on 18th November 1962. It must have been freezing. Just thinking about it sent shivers through my body. I salute all those brave men for their bravery.

The next morning, we left the guest house and walked towards the open field, where on one side is the Indian post, and on the opposite side, the Chinese area is clearly visible. First, we paid tribute at the War Memorial of the Gorkha Regiment in Chusul. After walking almost twenty kilometres, we finally reached the hallowed monument where the memorial to the 114 bravehearts of Rezang La was built. The last rites of all those 114 soldiers were also performed here. A hundred and fourteen stones from the battle site were brought here so that their memories could be preserved. The names of these heroes of the 13th Battalion of the Kumaon Regiment are inscribed in golden letters on the pages of history. We Indians can never repay the debt we owe these bravehearts.

As I paid homage to the brave men, my eyes became moist, and my heart was filled with immense respect. Recently, the National Book Trust, under their Veer Gatha series, has also brought out comics for children based on Maj Shaitan Singh's heroics so that future generations can learn about such great heroes and revere them. This is a welcome step. In memory of Maj Shaitan Singh, the Jodhpur Division of Indian Railways has named a station on the Jodhpur-Jaisalmer route as Shaitan Singh Nagar.

The words of poet Thomas Macaulay are inscribed on the monument at Rezang La:

> *'How can a man die better than facing fearful odds for the ashes of his fathers and the temples of his gods.'*

After visiting Leh in 2007, I had only one desire left to visit Tawang. That desire was fulfilled in October 2014. Following the war of 1962, the Aksai Chin and 42,735 square km portion of Arunachal Pradesh was seized by China. It is well known that this war proved to be the most fatal and disastrous for our country, in which we not only lost our valuable land but also a large number of our soldiers. It is said that the liability for this catastrophe lay with then Defence Minister Krishna Menon and our first Prime Minister Jawaharlal Nehru. Menon even closed down many of our munition factories, believing that India did not face a threat from any foreign power. Not only that, he also cut back on the defence budget. This immature thinking and omission on his part became the reason for our defeat. The war has left a deep wound which hasn't healed even after all these decades. Well, perhaps that was the destiny of our country. When China annexed Tibet in 1950, Vallabhbhai Patel wrote a long letter to Pandit Nehru, in which he warned that 'India should be cautious of China. A situation is arising where China can also attack India in the future.' Sardar Patel passed away in December 1950, and Nehru forgot his warning. If his warning had been acted upon immediately, the outcome of the 1962 war would have been different.

Apart from this, there were similar pointers in 1960 and 1961 as well that indicated that China could attack India at any time. But Pandit Nehru and Menon still disregarded them. Additionally, Menon's relations with the then Army Chief General Thimayya were also not cordial. The entire country had to bear the brunt of this remissness for decades and is bearing it even today. The state of the preparedness of our army was so abysmal that when they went to capture Goa in 1961, the men of one of the battalions were wearing canvas shoes. The Indian Army fought the China War with the .303 bolt action rifle used in the Second World War, whereas the Chinese Army already had modern guns like AK 47. In 2016, I came across Shiv Kunal Verma's book, *1962: The War that Wasn't,* in which that particular period has been described quite well. Verma's father served as a captain in the army in 1962. When one reads the book, one realizes how our brave soldiers had to face huge obstacles at every step because of the policies of Nehru and Menon.

Now let me take you to NEFA(North-East Frontier Agency), what today's Arunachal Pradesh was called then. It was the other area where battles of the 1962 war was fought. I had a desire to visit the battlefield since childhood. Finally, I had the opportunity in October 2014.

On 17th November 1962, when Chinese forces entered the battlefield of Nuranang, Rifleman Jaswant Singh Rawat of Garhwal Rifles, along with his other two comrades, Lance Naik Trilok Singh and Rifleman Gopal Singh, held their ground and thwarted the Chinese attack. In fact, when Chinese soldiers entered Bum La Pass, their troops also entered Arunachal from all three directions. A group that advanced towards Sela Pass was stopped there by Jaswant Singh and his comrades. The other Chinese troops had crossed the entire Arunachal and reached close to Tezpur in Assam. China lost 300 of its soldiers in this face-to-face combat. When they attacked for the fourth time, Jaswant Singh, who was going to pick up the machine gun of a dead Chinese soldier, was hit by a bullet and was seriously injured. It is said that Jaswant Singh single-handedly fought the Chinese continuously for 72 hours. The room where he used to live has been converted into a small temple. Even today, the bedsheet in his room is changed daily, and five soldiers are deployed twenty-four hours in his service. Considering he is alive, the Indian Army has given him six promotions so far. Every soldier and officer of the Indian Army, right from a common soldier to a general who passes through this region, does not move forward without saluting Rifleman-turned-Captain Jaswant Singh Rawat at his memorial.

Some bunkers here have still been conserved by the Indian Army. The phones, utensils, kitchen, stove, helmets, etc., used during the 1962 war are all preserved. Everything has been kept as it is. We also learnt that all the bunkers were prepared in just twenty-three days, as the Chinese troops started infiltrating in September 1962. That was the time when the Indian Army built these bunkers. There is no doubt that by attacking us in 1962, China had stabbed us in the back. However, the responsibility for losing the war does not lie with the Indian Army, but with the political pundits of our country, who trusted China and pushed the country into the vortex of such a terrible tragedy. After visiting all these places and analyzing them, I realized that our soldiers did not lack bravery, courage and valour; rather, they sacrificed their lives for the country with a smile. The war with China lasted for one month, after which China declared a unilateral ceasefire. In this war, 1,383 Indian soldiers made the supreme sacrifice, 1,047 were injured, 1,696 went missing, and 3,968 soldiers were taken as prisoners of war.

It became evident that the Indian soldiers were severely lacking in resources. They didn't even have warm clothes. Four soldiers shared a single blanket. More soldiers lost their lives to the inclement weather than in the attack by the Chinese. Not just warm clothes, the soldiers did not even have sufficient weaponry to fight with. The lack of weapons and the indifference of the defence minister and the prime minister towards the army were the main reasons for our defeat in 1962. It is also inconceivable why Pandit Nehru did not use the air force in this war when China's air power would have almost been exhausted by the time they reached Tibet. Later, this was confirmed by America, too.

After the war, when the outcome of the war was being discussed in the parliament, Nehru said that the area of 42,735 square km occupied by China was completely barren. Responding to this statement, an MP named Mahavir Tyagi sarcastically said, "Mr Nehru, I don't have any hair on my head. That, too, has become barren. Why not give that also to China?"

The border dispute, the root of all the trouble, started in 1914 when the British Government signed a treaty with China recognizing the McMahon Line. The 1949 communist government of China viewed this treaty with suspicion and evaded its full recognition, while India continued to think that China would fully adhere to the McMahon Line. When the Dalai Lama left Tibet and came to India in 1959, he entered India via Tawang. After spending a few days in Tawang, he went to Delhi, where Nehru welcomed him with open arms. China was stung by this. This should have alerted us. But our leaders continued their bonhomie with the Chinese leader. As if that was not enough, in 1960, Nehru also advocated making China a permanent member of the United Nations Security Council.

There is another small area in Arunachal Pradesh adjacent to the Chinese border. It is Tawang. Although it is small, it is very critical from a strategic point of view. China continues to assert its supremacy over Tawang, which was the focal point of the 1962 war. Fifty kilometres above Tawang, there is a place called Bum La, from where the Chinese land can be seen clearly. This is actually the LOAC (Line of Actual Control), which divides India and China.

During the 1962 war, this is the point where the Chinese soldiers entered and attacked India. Subedar Jogendra Singh, a valiant soldier of the 1 Sikh Regiment, was posted there. We have already discussed that in the 1962 war, we had a severe shortage of weapons and other resources. Here, too, the price for those insufficiencies had to be paid. On the morning of 23rd October 1962, China launched an attack in this area. They were larger in numbers than our soldiers, but the spirits of our soldiers were high. Sub Jogendra Singh did not lose his nerve even when there were only seventeen soldiers left defending the post. Raising the thunderous cry, "*Jo Bole so Nihal, Sat Shri Akal*", he kept moving forward undeterred. Blood was flowing from his body as he had also been shot in the thigh. He freed the Namka Chu post from the Chinese for a while but could not stop the second attack. When bullets and weapons ran out, he continued to kill Chinese soldiers with the bayonet of his gun. In the end, this brave soldier of Mother India laid down his life for the country. There is a memorial of Sub Jogendra Singh, where we paid homage during our visit.

Since the war, except for a few isolated incidents, not a single bullet has been fired here. The Indian Army has a conference room, guest house and a small auditorium here. Twice a year, Chinese soldiers hold feasts for Indian Army soldiers on 1st October and 30th October. That tent is pitched on a platform built in front of the Chinese area. The Indian Army invites the Chinese soldiers to its area on the 15th of August and 26th of January and hosts a feast for them, a tradition that has continued for many years now. A major on duty there told us that during the 1962 war, the Chinese Army had infiltrated into India from this area and launched the attack. A rock marks the dividing line between India and China here; it is called the 'Rock of Peace'. I was out of breath after walking just a little in Bum La, which is situated at an altitude of 16,000 feet. It also started snowing lightly and was terribly cold. We were surprised to see that China had constructed a paved road till the last post, while on the

Indian side, we had to make so much effort to reach here. A generator was the source of electricity for our men, which was available only till 3 p.m. Mobile connectivity was non-existent, and when we checked our mobiles, they were receiving Wi-Fi signals from the Chinese region. That simply meant that China was much ahead of us. On the other hand, we were not even able to maintain our roads to the border. All this made me quite sad. During my visit to Leh in 2007, I realized that the kind of development that the government has carried out on the border with Pakistan has a long way to go in this area. This is probably because Pakistan is perceived as a more dangerous enemy than China.

As were the guests of the army, we were seated in the army guest room and were served hot parathas with potato curry. Being able to have such delicious food at an altitude of 16,000 feet was no less than a dream. The hot tea infused our bodies with new energy. We proceeded to the war memorial at Tawang and paid tribute to the bravehearts before our departure from Arunachal Pradesh.

For their heroism in the 1962 war, Maj Shaitan Singh, Sub Sardar Jogendra Singh and Maj Dhan Singh Thapa were all awarded the Param Vir Chakra. The country salutes these brave men who fought selflessly for the nation.

A visit to regions like Chushul and Tawang at least once in one's lifetime is a must. It is no less than a pilgrimage as one sees first-hand how and under what circumstances our soldiers sacrificed their lives and how they continue to protect their motherland in the most unfavourable conditions.

8

The India-Pak War of 1965: Warriors in Tanks

The safety, honour and welfare of your country come first, always and every time. The honour, welfare and comfort of the men you command come next. Your own ease, comfort and safety come last, always and every time.

—Lord Philip Chetwode

In 1965, Pakistan attacked India, perhaps thinking that India was still reeling from the loss in the war with China in 1962. This misconception was further fuelled by Nehru's death in 1964. Pakistan thought that it was the right time to defeat India and merge Kashmir with Pakistan forever. Another reason was that in 1965, Pakistan. It was not only getting state-of-the-art weapons from America but also full support on every front. America had delivered a consignment of modern Patton tanks to Pakistan around that time, and the Indian tanks were nothing compared to them. In fact, India was still using Sherman tanks from the Second World War. At that time, Pakistan had a total of 756 tanks, out of which 352 were Patton tanks, whereas India had 608 tanks, out of which only 182 were Centurion tanks and the rest were Sherman tanks. Pakistan not only had tanks, but it also had more modern weapons at that point in time.

There is an old saying – 'The enemy of the enemy is a friend.' Bhutto proved this and set out to strengthen Pakistan's relations with China. Taking advantage of the acrimony in the India-China relations, he started making forceful efforts to sway China in favour of Pakistan. From then on, the proximity between Pakistan and China started increasing. Today, the state of affairs is such that Pakistan has even granted permission to China to build roads within its territory through Pakistan-occupied Kashmir. Moreover, to pursue its business interests, China has not only taken land from Pakistan at Gwadar Port but also directly connected it to Aksai Chin so that goods or crude oil arriving from the Gulf countries can be transported to China more swiftly and economically. Pakistan and China are executing all these projects under CPEC (China-Pakistan Economic Corridor). Subsequently, China wants to connect Pakistan's Karachi and Peshawar cities to Chinese territory.

However, it seems more likely that, as a pretext for these projects, China wants to keep an eye on and put pressure on India from a strategic point of view. Nevertheless, these activities are a matter of concern for India. India will have to decide its policy in this regard soon, and the government has started working in this direction. Recently, the government has started deploying BrahMos missiles on the India-China border, drawing flak from the Chinese.

In 1965, it was Pakistan's blunder that became its undoing. This war was said to be the brainchild of Pakistan's then Foreign Minister, Zulfikar Ali Bhutto. He convinced then-president Ayub Khan that if Pakistan attacked India at that time, then not only would the enemy be taught a lesson, but they could also capture Kashmir. Ayub Khan was swayed by Bhutto's idea. He also concurred that after losing the 1962 war, India would not have been able to amply restore its military capabilities and would be psychologically weak at that point.

Pakistan started this war by launching an attack on the Rann of Kutch. It wanted to assess how India would respond to the attack. It also wanted the focus of the Indian Army to shift to Kutch so that it could easily infiltrate into Kashmir. Pakistan first attacked the Sardar Post in Kutch. However, the Central Reserve Police Force defeated the Pakistanis in just a 12-hour-long battle. Even though Pakistan had more advanced tanks and fighter planes than India, all the plans of Pakistan were dashed owing to the valour of Indian soldiers. In many ways, this war was fought in a completely different manner than the battles earlier. For example, this was the first time the Indian Army was ordered to enter Pakistan and launch attacks. Our then Prime Minister Shri Lal Bahadur Shastri ordered that the enemy be given a befitting reply. In fact, when Army Chief J.N. Choudhary said that they would have to enter the enemy's territory and fight, Lal Bahadur Shastri told him to advance without any hesitation. This was also a bit strange because, till then, India had never violated the international border in any war.

India had Centurion and Sherman tanks that it had received from Britain, and most of them were from the Second World War era, whereas Pakistan brimmed with overconfidence because of the state-of-the-art Patton tanks it had received from America. However, Pakistan had no idea what destruction the Indian Army would bear upon those Patton tanks.

During the 1965 war, mainly the following officers displayed unprecedented bravery at the following places:

1. Haji Pir – Lieutenant General Ranjit Singh Dayal
2. Phillora – Lieutenant Colonel A.B. Tarapore and Major Bhupinder Singh
3. Asal Uttar – Company Quarter Master Havildar Abdul Hamid
4. Barki – Subedar Ajit Singh
5. Dograi – Lieutenant Colonel Desmond Hayde.

Haji Pir Pass was the entryway for the tribals being sent by Pakistan, and it was very crucial to close it. The responsibility of closing it was given to Lieutenant General Ranjit Singh Dayal of the Para Troopers.

(Ranjit Singh Dayal was a major during the 1965 war.) He discharged this responsibility very well. As the soldiers advanced towards their goal, they had to depend on biscuits and snacks for several days and cover a height of several thousand feet in adverse conditions. However, the soldiers under the leadership of Lt Gen Dayal did not give up and captured Haji Pir from the enemy. Lt Gen Dayal was awarded the Mahavir Chakra for his bravery. But in the end, under the Tashkent Declaration, both India and Pakistan had to vacate the areas occupied by each other. Our soldiers were most distraught when they had to leave Haji Pir because many of their comrades had sacrificed their lives to capture Haji Pir. It had been a hard battle. It is said that when the soldiers were asked to return, their eyes became moist as they recalled the martyrdom of their comrades.

The Indian tricolour was also hoisted at Barki, which was just about eighteen kilometres from Lahore. The credit for this goes to the efficient leadership of Subedar Ajit Singh. The Barki Memorial in Ferozepur was built in memory of the soldiers of the 7th Infantry Division who laid down their lives on the battlefield in 1965 and paved the way for the fall of Barki. It has a pillar in the centre, a Patton tank and a Barki mile stone at the south.

Here, it is absolutely necessary to mention Lieutenant Colonel A.B. Tarapore, who played a major role in the enemy's defeat. Tarapore was born on 19th August 1923 in Bombay. Tarapore of 17 Pune Horse received orders on 11th September 1965 to capture Phillora. Mounting his Centurion tank, he fought the enemy with great valour in the battle of Chawinda in Phillora in the Sialkot area of Pakistan. He and his team destroyed a total of sixty Pakistani tanks. Despite his wounds, Tarapore continued to fight until India achieved victory on the 14th of September. In the end, he made the supreme sacrifice for the country.

He was posthumously awarded the Param Vir Chakra. Tarapore was the senior officer who received the Param Vir Chakra at the age of forty-two. Major Bhupinder Singh was also awarded the Mahavir Chakra. Maj Bhupinder Singh belonged to the same armed regiment that has the distinction of destroying twenty-seven enemy tanks. Maj Singh was badly injured and later attained martyrdom. A colony in West Delhi has been named after him.

In Asal Uttar, it was Company Quarter Master Havildar Abdul Hamid who dug the grave for the enemy. He was born on 1st July 1933 in Dhampur in Ghazipur district of Uttar Pradesh. Abdul Hamid, who was 6 feet 2 inches tall, always wanted to work for the country. He worked as a tailor when, one day, an army recruitment camp was held in his village. It presented an opportunity he always wanted. It seemed as if his lifelong wish was fulfilled, as he regretted not being able to do anything for the country during the 1962 war. During the 1965 war, he was posted at the Thag La Ridge of NEFA. On 10th September 1965, he was sent to Asal Uttar in the Khem Karan sector with his regiment of 4 Grenadiers. He went there in his jeep, which was equipped with a mobile rocket launcher (RCL gun), which targeted the enemy's Patton tanks. It is said that he single-handedly destroyed seven enemy Patton tanks. Then, the enemy targeted him, and on the very same day, Abdul Hamid died in action and attained martyrdom. He was awarded the Param Vir Chakra for his supreme sacrifice.

The Indian Army has built a martyr's memorial in Asal Uttar, where Abdul Hamid died a martyr. Thousands of people visit his tomb every year to pay tribute to the braveheart. In 2015, Prime Minister Shri Narendra Modi also visited the memorial. Only sixty kilometres away from Amritsar, which is connected to all the major regions of the country, it is easily accessible. In Asal Uttar, the then Lieutenant General

Har Baksh Singh planned a clever strategy. He had canal water released in the fields of Asal Uttar; Pakistan's Patton tanks got stuck in them like toys. A graveyard of Patton tanks can still be seen in Bhikhiwind village near Asal Uttar, where about 97 captured Pakistani Patton tanks were lined up. Interestingly, the Battle of Asal Uttar was one of the largest tank battles fought during the 1965 war.

Similarly, the Indian Army achieved success in Dograi under the leadership of Lieutenant Colonel Desmond Hayde of 3 Jat. Dograi ranks among the intense battles fought by the Indian Army during the war. Hayde personally encouraged every soldier, which had such a profound impact that each of his soldiers was willing to die for the country. Lt Col Hayde said only two things to his soldiers,

"Not a single man will retreat" and,

"Dead or alive, we will meet in Dograi!"

It had such a huge impact that every soldier fought that battle in a blind rage. Victory was to be achieved at any cost. And that is exactly what happened. Lt Col Desmond Hayde was awarded the Mahavir Chakra. Post-retirement, he settled down in Kotdwar. He also composed a song for children:

Another eminent personality who was born in Ludhiana was Kartar Singh Sarabha. A big statue of Kartar Singh Sarabha has been installed on the main GT Road. After paying homage to him in 2016, we travelled towards Khem Karan and Asal Uttar. I kept thinking about the war fought here and how India destroyed Pakistan's powerful Patton tanks. I thought about how the brave Abdul Hamid carried out the heroic act without any concern for his life. While pondering over these things, I saw an iron bridge in front of me. I asked my driver, "Is this Harike?"

He said, "Yes, it is."

I asked him to park the car and got out of the car to view the river from the bridge. I saw two rivers merging to become one. The Beas River meets the Sutlej River here. I was thrilled to see this confluence. Vyas River originates from Vyas Kund, which is in Rohtang Pass of Himachal Pradesh, and the water in this river is considered extremely sacred. While returning from our Ladakh trip, we visited and took a sip of the holy water at Vyas Kund. I have a special interest in locating the sources of rivers and the places where they merge into the sea. Till now, I have had the joy of seeing where the Ganga, Yamuna, Beas, Narmada and Indus originate from, to places of their confluence.

We crossed Harike and reached the tomb of the valiant Abdul Hamid. This was the same area around Cheema village where Abdul Hamid completely turned the battle around. After paying homage, we went to India's last border post at Khem Karan – BOP (Border Observation Post) 191, built by the Border Security Force. I had goosebumps when I climbed the tower and viewed the entire area. I marvelled at how our soldiers keep vigil here day and night. Barely a hundred yards ahead of that post was Pakistan's border post, where their flag was raised. At that time, we were at the last point of the last road in India, which was blocked with mud and bricks. It is also the starting point of the Kasur district of Pakistan.

India has fenced the border with barbed wire to prevent any incident of infiltration. At night, Section 144 is implemented in the entire area, and electric current starts flowing through the barbed wires. Despite such vigilance, narcotics and weapons are seized here every day. In the 1990s, barbed wire had not been installed, and that was how hapless Sarabjit entered the border of Pakistan and was forced to live a dreadful life in the Kot Lakhpat Jail of Lahore for twenty-two years. I saw the film Sabarjit, which is about his life. It shook me and made me think about how heartlessly and brutally Pakistan had treated an innocent common man like Sarabjit and destroyed his life. We were to travel to Amritsar via Bhikhiwind, which was Sarabjit's village. After seeing the barbed wire and remembering Sarabjit, I decided to go to Sarabjit's house, meet his brave sister, Dalbir Kaur, and salute her courage and bravery. She had left no stone unturned to rescue Sarabjit, but unfortunately, he was murdered by fellow inmates.

After seeing this post, we went to the dargah of a Pir or a saint, which is situated on No Man's Land, i.e., Zero Line. The name of this Pir is Pir Sheikh Brahm. Not only Indians but also Pakistanis come here to offer prayers. The white pillar dividing India and Pakistan is just a few steps away from here.

It is said that Guru Nanak Dev also visited this dargah before he journeyed to Mecca. For the first time in my life, I saw a dargah where huge bells were installed. When my friend Paramjit struck the bells, the sound pierced the silence and created a different kind of spell. People are allowed to visit only on Thursdays. However, a big lamp kept here burns continuously. After visiting a few more strategic areas, we went to Sarabjit's house in Bhikhiwind village. We met his sister-in-law at his house. She told us that the entire family had gone to Jalandhar. She also told us that after the release of the film, people from Mumbai, Kolkata and other far-off places had been visiting their houses. We prayed for the family in our hearts and set out for Amritsar.

This saga will be incomplete if the Air Force Chief during the 1965 war is not mentioned. During 1965, the Air Force was headed by Sardar Arjan Singh. Air Chief Marshal Arjan Singh was born on 15th April 1919 in Lyallpur, Punjab (present-day Faisalabad, Pakistan). He received his early education in a place called Montgomery in British India (present-day Pakistan). In 1938, he was admitted to the RAF (Royal Air Force)

College, Cranwell, and was commissioned as a pilot officer in 1939. Sardar Arjan Singh was the Chief of the Indian Air Force (Chief of Air Staff) from 1st August 1964 to 15th July 1969. Given his significant contribution during the India-Pakistan War of 1965, he was appointed the first Air Chief Marshal of India in January 2002. He was also the Lieutenant Governor of Delhi from December 1989 to December 1990. Under his leadership, the Indian Air Force performed its best in the 1965 war and played a decisive role in winning the war. They were the first to strike the Pakistani Patton tanks and provided close air support to the troops on the ground.

Another interesting account is that of an officer who was injured in the 1965 war. He not only wrote a new epic tale of patriotism but has also become a superhero for today's generation. His name is Major Harpal Singh Ahluwalia. Maj Ahluwalia was a member of the first Indian team that conquered Everest. On 29 May 1965, he conquered Everest, and in September 1965, he received orders to join the war. Maj Ahluwalia demonstrated immense courage and fought fiercely with the enemy. Unfortunately, an enemy bullet hit his spinal cord, as a result of which he has been in a wheelchair since then. With his liveliness and fortitude, he not only accepted this challenge but also established the Indian Spine Injury Hospital in Vasant Kunj, Delhi, where such patients are treated. Because of his dynamism and adventurous spirit, he has been awarded the Padma Bhushan, Padmashree and Arjuna Awards. Maj Ahluwalia has written thirteen books so far. I read his autobiography, *Higher than Everest,* in 1998, and since then, I have become his admirer. I have had the privilege of meeting him personally thrice. Moreover, my second book, *Atulya Bharat Ki Khoj,'* was also released by this great personality. In the Indo-Pak war of 1965, 3,293 soldiers made the supreme sacrifice, which included 179 officers, 130 junior commissioned officers, and

2,984 soldiers. Pakistan captured approximately 540 square km area of India, while the Indian Army captured 1,940 square km area of Pakistan. It was a battle where the Indian Army showed exemplary fortitude.

I can only say this to the bravehearts:

"We shall remember you with every rising sun and always salute you."

9

The India-Pak War of 1971: Men who birthed a Nation

If a man says he is not afraid of dying, he is either lying or he is a Gurkha.

—Field Marshal Sam Manekshaw

The 1971 war was, in a way, the result of Pakistan's oppression and exploitation of the people from its own country – East Pakistan. At the beginning of 1971, the atrocities of the Pakistani rulers on East Pakistan had increased so much that it was beyond the capacity of the people to bear them. They started migrating to India. The migration was on such a large scale that it rattled the economy of West Bengal, Manipur, Assam and other north-eastern states of India. The chief ministers of those states repeatedly requested the Prime Minister to solve the problem. Although the Indian Government provided accommodation and food to the refugees, the sudden influx of ten lakh refugees was a matter of concern. On 3rd March 1971, a curfew was imposed in Dhaka, and Lieutenant General Tikka Khan of the Pakistan Army was appointed as the martial law administrator. It is said that Tikka Khan carried out the second Jallianwala Bagh carnage there, due to which he earned the epithet 'Butcher of Bengal'. The Pakistani Army started massacring the people. Intellectuals were selectively targeted and killed.

At that time, the Chief of the Indian Army was Sam Manekshaw, who was counted among the best military officers in India. He was called by the then Prime Minister Indira Gandhi, who told him to enter East Pakistan and launch an attack. Manekshaw responded, saying that it was not possible. He said, "If we attack now, we may lose the war, and I fight to win the war, not to lose it."

Indira Gandhi did not expect this response from him. But when Manekshaw argued, "Monsoon is around the corner. At that time, all the rivers and streams there will be in a spate. Our soldiers will not be able to deal with those conditions fittingly."

So, Indira ji asked, "When will we be in a position to attack?" Sam replied, "'By November."

Indira Gandhi gave him her consent. Meanwhile, the army started its preparations in full swing. In East Pakistan, the Mukti Vahini, a guerilla movement under the leadership of Mujibur Rahman, was fighting the Pakistani Army. The rulers of Pakistan wanted to impose their culture on East Pakistan. They wanted to make Urdu the chief language in place of Bengali. This riled the Bengali majority of East Pakistan and became the main reason for the conflict. The atrocities committed by Pakistani soldiers were on the rise.

On 3rd December 1971, the Pakistani Air Force simultaneously attacked several air bases in India. The major ones among them were Amritsar, Pathankot, Srinagar, Avantipur, Uttarlai, Jodhpur, Ambala and Agra. India was already prepared. The Indian Army was waiting for Pakistan to attack so that they could give a befitting reply. And that is exactly what happened – the attacks were carried out. This war was imposed upon India. Pakistan's internal strife had escalated to such an extent that it was unable to curb it. The reason for internal trouble was the widespread support that Mujibur Rahman's party received in East Pakistan, which the rulers did not like. As soon as Pakistan launched the attacks, the Indian Army sprang into action, and the war began.

In this war, the soldiers had to defend both our eastern and western borders simultaneously. But their enthusiasm was unprecedented, and their morale was high. By now, Prime Minister Indira Gandhi had decided that East Pakistan would be made an independent country. She called upon Manekshaw and all the military officers to give their all for this. She gave a message to the people through All India Radio and said that the war had been imposed on India and that we would give a befitting reply to it. The entire country united and stood behind Mrs Gandhi.

The morale of the army led by Sam Manekshaw was always going to be high. Sam's full name was Hormusji Framji Jamshedji Manekshaw. He was born to a Parsi family on 3rd April 1914 in Amritsar. His father was a doctor by profession who settled in Amritsar in the year 1900. All his children – Sam and his siblings, could speak English, Hindi, Gujarati and Punjabi fluently.

Sam wanted to become a doctor and wanted to go abroad to study like his elder brothers. But destiny had something else in store for him. He appeared for the army examination and was selected for the first batch of the Indian Military Academy. During the Second World War, Sam was sent to Burma to fight against the Japanese. The seven bullets fired by the Japanese at him hit him in his stomach, lungs, kidney and liver. He was seriously injured. Seeing his bravery, his commanding officer hung the Military Cross on his chest on the battlefield itself, which was the highest medal for bravery at that time. Sam's commanding officer did so because, at that time, the soldiers who made the supreme sacrifice were not awarded this medal. The medical officer of the regiment sent him to the hospital in Pegu. The Russian doctor there threw up his hands. But Sam's assistant, Sher Singh, did not give up and requested that the doctors save Sam. Sher Singh did not want to hear 'no' from the doctor under any circumstances. The doctor was stunned to see that Sam was still conscious thirty-six hours after being seriously injured. When he asked Sam what had happened to him, Sam replied that a mule had kicked him in the stomach. The doctor admired Sam's humorous attitude in that grave condition. He immediately performed the surgery. In this way, Sam received a new life from God early in his career. His life was saved due to the tireless efforts of Sher Singh. In 1961, the then Defence Minister V.K. Krishna Menon did not share cordial relations with the Army Chief and other officers. He decided to teach Manekshaw a lesson. At that time, Manekshaw was the Commandant at Wellington College, Nilgiris. Menon had already made up his mind to court-martial him and appointed an inquiry committee against him. But before a decision could be reached, China attacked India in 1962, and it was Menon who had to lose his post. In an interview, Manekshaw is seen speaking humorously about how the Chinese had arrived to save him. Imagine if an officer like Manekshaw had been removed from the army at that time; what huge losses the country would have suffered!

As he climbed the stairs of success, Sam was appointed the Chief of the Army Staff in 1969. After India won the 1971 war, Sam was awarded the Padma Vibhushan. In 1973, he had the honour of being appointed the First Field Marshal of India. Apart from this, he was also conferred many other military awards. Sam spent the last years of his life in Coonoor in the Nilgiris. He was the commandant in Wellington for many years, and perhaps that is why he fell in love with the Nilgiri hills.

Sam departed for his heavenly abode on 27th June 2007 at the age of ninety-four. Today, his huge statue stands at the entrance of the Military College, Wellington. In January 2016, I had the honour of visiting Wellington and Sam's statue. My heart felt at peace when I paid obeisance to this brave man at his *karmbhoomi*.

During the 1971 war, to divert India's attention from the eastern front, Pakistan started moving its army beyond Jaisalmer towards Longewala. Pakistan's strategy was that since India had deployed its entire military power in Bangladesh, it would surreptitiously attack the western border, capture it, and force India to retreat from Bangladesh. From 4th to 7th December 1971, Pakistan continued its attacks on this front, to which the Indian Army gave a befitting reply. Only a hundred and twenty Indian soldiers were deployed in the Longewala sector, whereas Pakistan had 65 T-59 tanks supplied by China and a large army of 2,000 soldiers.

But the morale of the Indian soldiers was very high. Major Kuldeep Singh Chandpuri of the Punjab Regiment was posted at Longewala, and Lieutenant Dharamveer was posted at Sadewala, which was seventeen kilometres away. The Pakistani Army attacked at night because they knew that the air force could not be used at that hour. Therefore, it was crucial for India to somehow hold back the Pakistani Army till morning. If Maj Kuldeep Singh Chandpuri and Lt Dharamveer had not stalled the Pakistani Army, it would have reached Jaisalmer airstrip before morning, and we would probably have never witnessed the job done by the Indian Air Force. From this, you can comprehend how crucial this mission was. The Border Security Force also played a significant role in this mission.

With its unparalleled bravery and valour, the 23 Punjab Regiment accomplished this seemingly impossible task. Because of this courageous act, Maj Kuldeep Singh Chandpuri was awarded the Mahavir Chakra. The Indian Air Force also did a wonderful job in this war. Squadron Leader Ravindranath Bali, M.S. Bawa, Squadron Leader Dilip Kumar Das and Flight Lieutenant Ramesh Chandra Gosain, along with their colleagues, carried out precise bombing from the planes, which unnerved the enemy. Within a few hours, the Indian Air Force changed the dynamics of the entire war. Pakistan, with its 2,000 soldiers, planned to have breakfast at Longewala, lunch at Ramgarh, and dinner at Jaisalmer. Its plans were crushed by the brave men of the Indian Air Force. Pakistan's dreams bit the dust. Pakistan wouldn't have anticipated that the powerful T-59 tanks that it received from China would be shattered by the Indian Air Force. The brave Indian air troops destroyed 34 tanks of Pakistan. In this war that lasted from 4th to 7th December 1971, Kuldeep Singh Chandpuri, Commanding Officer of the Punjab Regiment, played a vital role. Bhuj was the main operation centre of the Air Force command. The 23 Punjab Regiment was awarded with battle honours. Famous filmmaker J.P. Dutta made a film on the 1971 war – *Border*. The character played by Sunny Deol in this film was based on Maj Kuldeep Singh Chandpuri. With his unparalleled bravery, he foiled the Pakistani Army's plan. Maj Chandpuri passed away in 2018.

The temple of Tanot Mata also plays a special role in the war. The temple is near the border. By the grace of the goddess, none of the bombs dropped by the Pakistanis in this region exploded. Those bombs are still intact in the temple. The soldiers of the Border Security Force deployed there at that time believed that their lives and those of all the people in the area were saved by the grace of the Mother Goddess, and the temple was looked after by the BSF personnel. There is also a rest house in the same yard, where guests of the Border Security Force can stay. I had this privilege in the year 2012. We spent the night and attended the first *aarti* of the morning. The soldiers present there told us the stories of the 1965 and 1971 war and also showed us the intact bombs.

After breakfast, we went to the international border, which is just twelve kilometres from the temple. We strolled along the international border quite leisurely and talked to the local soldiers. Common Indian citizens are prohibited from visiting this area. I have had several opportunities to see India's international border/Line of Control/Line of Actual Control with Pakistan and China. Among them, the India-Bangladesh border area in Cherrapunji, Leh, Dras, Kargil, Akhaura, Dawki, Chushul, Nadabet, Siachen, Badmer, Ferozepur, Fazilka, Khem Karan, Kutch, Attari, and Bum La Pass in Tawang are prominent. But this was the first time I saw the international border from the sandy landscape of Rajasthan. After that, we went to the Longewala sector, where we paid homage to the bravehearts at the war memorial. The T-59 tanks that were destroyed by the Indian Army are still displayed there. We climbed on them and took pictures with great pride. Who would not be proud of their country and the brave soldiers?

During the same 1971 war, a twenty-one-year-old young man brought glory to the tricolour when he risked his life in the battle that was fought in the plains of Jammu and Kashmir and the Basantar river area. The name of that young army officer was Second Lieutenant Arun Khetrapal. He had joined the army only six months earlier but his spirits were high.

Pakistanis also know the Battle of Basantar as the Battle of Bada Pind. Arun Khetrapal was born on 14th October 1950, in Pune. When he joined the army, he was given command of 17 Horse, Pune. The security of this area was very important to him because the Jammu and Punjab roads intersected at this place. Second Lt Arun attacked Pakistani soldiers with his tank and, one by one, destroyed four enemy tanks. After some time, a shell hit his tank, causing his tank to catch fire. When his commanding officer called him to retreat, Second Lt Arun said, "My gun is still working, and as long as it is working, I will continue to target the enemy!"

That is how valiant he was. But he sustained severe injuries and died a martyr. Khetrapal was honoured with Param Vir Chakra, the highest gallantry award. In this battle, the Poona Horse of India and the Lancers Regiment of Pakistan came face-to-face. Incidentally, before independence both these regiments were part of the united Bombay Cavalry.

On 29th June 2016, I met the family of Captain Vijayant Thapar, who made the supreme sacrifice in Kargil. Vijayant had in Kargil on the same day – 29th June in the year 1999. I learnt from his father, Colonel V.N. Thapar, that Vijayant had considered Arun Khetrapal his idol and that he had visited his house in Delhi many times. Look at how destiny works! Like Arun Khetrapal, Vijayant also died a martyr's death in the war at the young age of twenty-two. At that time, he had been in the army for only six months as well. Another coincidence was that both Arun and Vijayant's fathers and grandfathers were army officers. It was such a strange coincidence.

Another interesting fact is that to date, the Indian Air Force has received the Param Vir Chakra only once, and it was awarded to none other than Flying Officer Nirmal Jit Singh Sekhon. He was born on 17th July 1945 in Ludhiana, Punjab. His father was also in the Indian Air Force. Since childhood, Nirmal Jit had dreamed of flying a plane. That dream turned into a passion, and Sekhon became a fighter pilot in the air force. During the 1971 war, he was posted at Srinagar Air Base. Pakistan had made nefarious plans to attack Srinagar Air Base. Pakistan had planned to fly low to the mountains of Poonch and then elevate their fighter planes to 16,000 feet right at Poonch. They were aware that they would appear on the radar of the Indian Air Force only after Poonch and that by then, the Indian Air Force would not even get a chance to pull itself together because the distance from Poonch to Srinagar was only six minutes. With this plan, they launched their attack on the Srinagar Air Base on 14th December 1971.

Pakistan's plan was successful to some extent as our radars could not detect the aircrafts due to the sudden attack but for India, it was a 'do or die' situation because it was necessary to defend Srinagar Air Base at any cost.

Six modern Sabre jet aircraft of the enemy were hovering overhead and firing. Meanwhile, a young Sikh managed to reach his plane. He started targeting Pakistani planes as soon as he took off. In no time, this led to a commotion in the enemy camp. They had no idea that something like this could happen. Nirmal Jit Singh Sekhon destroyed two enemy aircraft. But then Sekhon's plane caught fire. He was ejected from the plane with his parachute, but he could not survive and died a martyr. He was posthumously awarded the Param Vir Chakra for his heroism. The Indian Air Force Museum, situated in Palam, Delhi, houses the 'GNAT' plane flown by Nirmal Jit Singh Sekhon and his statue. I bowed my head in reverence. There is also a war memorial in its yard. This museum is unique and one of its kind in India. In this museum, the uniforms used by the Indian Air Force from its inception (1932) till today, as well as many historical photos, weapons, and information about the bravehearts, are on display. Most notably, the aircraft used during the First World War, the Second World War, and the Indo-Pakistan wars of 1971 and 1999, such as Douglas, NOT, Canberra and MIG, can be seen. The pieces of Pakistan's aircraft that were destroyed by India are also on display. After paying tribute to the bravehearts, I felt humbled.

Delhi has the most famous and iconic war memorial in the country. It is the India Gate. This forty-three-metre-high monument is situated on Rajpath, India's most important road, and is made of red and yellow sandstone. It was built in 1931 in memory of approximately 10,000 Indian soldiers who were killed during the First World War and the Afghan War. The names of a total of 13,300 bravehearts, including

British army officers, are inscribed on the walls of this memorial. This monument was inspired by the Arc de Triomphe of Paris, which is a tribute to the men who fought and died for France during the Revolutionary and Napoleonic Wars. It was designed by Edwin Lutyens, the famous English architect.

The Amar Jawan Jyoti had been installed in the four corners of a platform below the main memorial in memory of the soldiers who had made the supreme sacrifice in the India-Pakistan War of 1971; it was continuously aflame. As a mark of respect to the soldiers who had made the supreme sacrifice, a gun was placed upside down, with a helmet hanging on it. Every year on 26th January, the Prime Minister and the Defence Minister of India, along with the three army chiefs, pay tribute and homage to the bravehearts. When India Gate was completed, a statue of George V was also installed there, which was later shifted to Coronation Park in 1968. The lawns of India Gate are known for their greenery and expanse, where hundreds of people gather every day.

For the past many years, there had been a discussion on building a memorial, which would be purely dedicated to Indian soldiers. The National War Memorial near India Gate, was inaugurated in 2019 by Prime Minister Narendra Modi. It has the names of the bravehearts written in golden letters, along with the busts of some of the heroes. The Amar Jawan Jyoti, previously at the India Gate, has merged with the new flame there. A museum dedicated to the heroes of the battles of Independent India is also in the pipeline. A fitting tribute to the country's bravehearts indeed.

Another hero from the 1971 war is Major Hoshiar Singh. He was born on 5th May 1936 in the Sonipat district of Haryana. He was very valiant, and from 15th to 17th December 1971, he was deployed in the area near the Basantar River in the Shakargarh sector. The Pakistani Army attacked this area three times in a row. But Hoshiar Singh and his brave comrades foiled the attacks every single time. It is said that during the war, Hoshiar Singh would go to every soldier and encourage him without caring for his life. Due to his encouragement, the soldiers gave it their all. Meanwhile, Maj Hoshiar Singh was gravely injured. But neither did he lose courage nor did he leave his soldiers. He was awarded the Param Vir Chakra for his bravery and valour. They finally left the field only after the ceasefire was declared. Maj Hoshiar Singh fiercely fought the Pakistanis in both the wars of 1965 and 1971. Maj Singh rose to the post of brigadier and retired. He finally left for his heavenly abode on 6th December 1998.

In the 1971 war, another valiant soldier, who was also a gifted hockey player, was awarded the Param Vir Chakra. He was Lance Naik Albert Ekka. During the 1971 war, Ekka was posted in the Gangasagar area. A resident of Gumla, Jharkhand, he fought the enemy with exemplary courage. The battle in which he fought and made the supreme sacrifice was crucial, and led the way for the Indian troops into Bangladesh, eventually creating the new nation.

The War of 1971 was a war in which all three branches of the military fought actively and wrote a saga of bravery. After the army and air force, it is imperative to mention the navy. During the war, the then Navy Chief Admiral Nanda met Indira Gandhi and requested that the navy should also be allowed to prove its worthiness in this war. Indira Gandhi gave him the freedom to act as he wished. Grabbing the opportunity, Admiral Nanda devised such a strategy that the Pakistani Navy not only suffered losses worth billions of rupees but also one-third of its navy was almost destroyed. India was very well aware that if Pakistan's Karachi port was destroyed, then the Pakistani Navy would never be able to reach East Pakistan with aid. This strategy was executed by Admiral Nanda and his brave officers. Operation Trident was put in motion, and not only

Pakistan's ships but also the oil tankers parked at Pakistan's Karachi port were set on fire. These small ships were equipped with missiles and sent towards Karachi from the Kutch and Bombay ports. To avoid any issues with fuel, these small ships were tied to the bigger ships and taken to a place little before Karachi. It would be interesting to mention here that all the officers of the Indian Navy were speaking in Russian (they had recently undergone training in Russia), which the Pakistanis could not understand. So, they did not even get a whiff of India's plan. When the Indian Navy first struck, Pakistan thought that the Indian Air Force had attacked them. But by the time they could comprehend the situation, there was utter destruction.

One of these frigate ships was INS *Khukri,* captained by Mahendra Nath Mulla. The extremely fearless and resolute Mahendra Nath Mulla was born on 15th May 1926 in Gorakhpur. *Khukri* was a Blackwood class anti-submarine frigate built in England in 1950. It was deployed in Diu. On the night of 9th December 1971, *Khukri* became the target of a torpedo fired by an enemy submarine and caught fire. A hundred and seventy-six sailors and eighteen officers lost their lives in the incident. It is said that when the ship was sinking, Captain Mulla was standing on its deck smoking a cigarette nonchalantly. He had made up his mind that, in line with the highest traditions of the navy, he would sacrifice his life with the sinking ship. And that is exactly what happened. Captain Mulla was posthumously awarded the Mahavir Chakra. On the one hand, the navy celebrated the destruction of Karachi; on the other hand, it deeply mourned the loss of its hundred and ninety-four soldiers. That was the first and only incident after 1947, in which our warship fell prey to an enemy torpedo and sank. The Khukri Memorial was built in Diu in the memory of the brave soldiers. In 2011, I had the good fortune to pay homage at the memorial, which has a scaled model of INS Khukri enclosed in a glass case. The names of all the officers and sailors of the ship are etched so that their supreme sacrifice is never forgotten.

The war lasted from 3rd December to 16th December. In just thirteen days, India brought Pakistan down to its knees. Pakistan had to face a crushing defeat in this war. Pakistan's Lieutenant General Niazi signed the surrender letter with India's Lieutenant General Arora. Approximately 93,000 Pakistani soldiers had to surrender before the Indian Army in the Race Course area of Dhaka. This was the most disgraceful incident in the history of Pakistan and the most glorious in the history of the Indian Army. While talking about the creation of Bangladesh, it would not be fair if we did not talk about Major General J.R.F. Jacob since Jacob was the one who forced Niazi to kneel before India. Jacob was a Parsi who was born in Calcutta. He played a vital role in the Second World War and the India-Pakistan War of 1965. After he retired from the army, he served as the governor of Goa and Punjab. He died in January 2016, at the age of ninety-two in New Delhi.

Chief of the Army Staff Sam Manekshaw had created history with his troops. Indira Gandhi emerged as an Iron Lady in front of the world and announced on All India Radio:

"Today, another nation has been born on the world map, and its name is 'Bangladesh.'"

The Bangladeshi people had won, and the armed struggle of Mukti Bahini had yielded the expected results. However, there was a price to pay, as there always is in any war. In this entire conflict, about ten lakh Bangladeshis lost their lives, and about a crore people took refuge in India.

About 2,500 soldiers made the supreme sacrifice in this war, and 93,000 Pakistani soldiers were taken as prisoners of war by the Indian Army. Despite taking 93,000 Pakistani soldiers as prisoners of war, we did not gain anything at the negotiating table, i.e., the Shimla Agreement.

We could have used the situation to our advantage. It could have been a golden opportunity that could have been utilized very well for sorting out old blunders like Kashmir and Siachen, among others. That is why our intellectuals and war experts say that whatever we won in the 1971 war, we lost it all on the negotiating table.

10

The India-Pak Kargil War of 1999: *Yeh Dil Mange More*

Either I will come back after hoisting the tricolour, or I will come back wrapped in it, but I will be back for sure.

—Captain Vikram Batra

So far, India and Pakistan have fought four wars –1947, 1965, 1971 and 1999, and Pakistan has lost every single one of them. But what was appalling was when in the year 1999, on one hand, while the Prime Minister of India went to Lahore for peace talks, on the other, at the very same time, Pakistan stabbed us in the back. Since 1947, there was a tacit agreement between the two countries that they would not deploy their troops in the Kargil, Drass and Batalik regions during winter, which continued till May 1999. On 3rd May 1999, however, Tashi Namgyal, a Buddhist shepherd in Kargil, saw that some armed men had entered the Indian border. He immediately informed the Army. The Indian Army directly sent one of its search teams led by Captain Saurabh Kalia to the mountains. But that squad never returned, and horrifying what came back were their mutilated bodies. There was a wave of anger not only in the Indian Army but also in the entire country. Then, it was confirmed that Pakistan had encroached upon our territory with devious intentions and occupied it illegally. It is said that Pakistan deceitfully captured India's posts which had been left vacant during winter (The Economic Times, 25 July 2019) spread over 160 square kilometres. Now, you may call it a failure of our intelligence agencies or bad luck, but the worst has already taken place. We had no option but to challenge the enemy sitting on top of the hill, destroy them, and take back every inch of our land. Pakistan's goal was to capture the national highway going from Srinagar to Leh so that Leh and then Siachen could be captured next. This was what Pakistan had hoped to achieve in 1947 and 1965, too.

The Kargil War formally lasted for two months. At that time, I was a twenty-four-year-old youth, and my blood was boiling, like every other ordinary Indian's. During that time, on the morning of 23rd July 1999, I reached Jammu to visit Amarnath. This means that there were still three days left before the war ended. By then, our valiant soldiers had won back all the areas occupied by Pakistan. Drass was the epicentre of the war, which is about sixty-four kilometres from Kargil. The distance from Amarnath Base Camp (Baltal) to Drass is about forty-eight kilometres. During that time, some of our friends went ahead to Drass to see the horrors that had happened during the war, but I could not go. But I vowed that one day, I would definitely visit the holy lands of Drass and Kargil and pay obeisance. My dream finally came true in July 2007.

Our plan for the Leh trip was finalized on 5th July 2007. I called my friend, Rajiv Badu, who lives in Jammu and discussed the road route from Leh to Srinagar with him in detail because I knew that he was well aware of that route. Those days, the uncle of my childhood friend Gaurav Pathak was serving as the lieutenant general in the Gorkha Regiment. I discussed the broad outline of my trip with him. He immediately made arrangements for our stay at the Indian Army's guest house in Leh. In addition, he also made arrangements for our stay in Kargil (which was the epicentre of the India-Pakistan War of 1999). I would get goosebumps just thinking about whether I would ever be able to pay homage on the soil of Kargil, Drass, and Mushkoh Valley, where our brave soldiers sacrificed their lives for the country.

Finally, I took a flight from Indira Gandhi International Airport to Leh on 5th July 2007 along with my two friends, Gaurav Pathak and Tarun Malhotra. The duration of the flight from Delhi to Leh was only one hour and five minutes. Half an hour after the flight took off, the plane was above the mountains of Manali. Suddenly there was intense activity in the plane because the snow-covered peaks of Manali looked alluring.

Some foreign tourists were astounded and excited. Every passenger took as many photographs from as many angles as he could. Everyone was filled with joy upon seeing such a tranquil, endless, natural and unprecedented beauty of nature. Shortly after seeing the snow- covered peaks of Manali, we saw the brown, bare and rocky mountains. We realized that we were hovering above Leh and we proceeded to land.

At the airport, two soldiers from the Indian Army received us, and we immediately proceeded to the army guest house. Leh's climate is exceptional, and the crisp and clean air hit us. Rarely seen anywhere else in the country, there was no pollution in the air. By now, we realized that what we had heard about Leh seemed to be true. After fifteen minutes, we reached the army guest house. The guest house is situated in the army cantonment area on the banks of River Sindhu. Since Leh is situated at an altitude of approximately 11,562 feet above sea level, visitors are advised to rest and take it slow for the first day to acclimatize themselves.

After resting for a couple of hours, we decided to visit the local sights of Leh. A war memorial was built here after the 1962 war with China. We first went there and paid homage to the bravehearts. There were two epicentres of the 1962 war. One was Leh and the other was Tawang in Arunachal Pradesh which I visited in October 2014.

After spending two days in Leh, we left for Kargil-Drass. After travelling for about two hours, we entered the Batalik sector. Batalik was one of the main centres of the Kargil War of 1999. Captain Manoj Pandey, who was from Lucknow, was posthumously awarded the Param Vir Chakra for displaying unprecedented bravery and indomitable courage in the Zuber Top area of the Batalik sector during the war.

His words are well-known even today.

"If death strikes before I prove my blood, I swear, I will kill death!"

— Captain Manoj Kumar Pandey

(1/11 Gorkha Rifles)

Then we went to NH-1. There, we saw a board on which it was written: 'Beware, the enemy is watching you.' Limbu told us that there was a Pakistani post right in front and that they could see us from there. Limbu was a soldier of the Indian Army who was our guide. We took a photograph. I was filled with excitement. There was a very beautiful spring nearby, and its water was sweet and cool. It was probably the first time in my life that I had seen such a beautiful spring. That scene comes alive in front of my eyes even today.

After about an hour, we entered Kargil. It was an emotional moment for me because it was the same place where our countless soldiers made supreme sacrifices for the pride of our country. We were given a room in the guest house of the Gorkha Regiment of the Indian Army. In the evening, we met the Commanding Officer. He is a very lively person. He sent us to the Kala Pahar outpost with his vehicle and driver. Kala Pahar outpost is the last outpost of India, and one can see the Pakistani side. This place had gained fame during the 1965 war. It was great to see that even at this last post, a TV and dish antenna were installed for our soldiers. The experience of viewing the international border while having tea and hot pakoras was quite an experience.

The soldiers on duty told us that all the soldiers there greeted each other with 'Jai Mata Di'. When I asked why, I learnt that there was a small temple of Mata Sheronwali on the hill. During the 1965 war, when only a hundred soldiers were left at this post, Mata Sheronwali appeared in a dream and said, "Attack!"

Our soldiers obeyed her command, attacked the Pakistanis and chased away about five hundred Pakistani soldiers. Later, it was revealed that the Pakistanis had seen not a hundred but several thousand Indian soldiers. A red flag fluttered, on which '*Om*' was printed on one side and Hanumanji's figure on the other.

I learnt that this flag was displayed at all the forward posts of India as Indian soldiers are very religious. After some time, we returned to the mess and freshened up. I remember the movie *Don 2* playing on TV that day. I fixed my handycam and still cameras because the next day, we were to go to the most important place in this tour – Drass, which was the foremost centre of the Kargil War.

The next day started quite early, at 5 a.m. We set out for a morning walk to enjoy the morning view and the weather. We felt our bodies infused with wonderful energy as we breathed in the crisp cool air. We had our breakfast at around 8 a.m. and then set out on our journey. A major from the Indian Army was deployed to make us familiar with the tough terrain of the area. Our lunch, four folding chairs, and a small table were packed and loaded into the vehicle. After travelling for a while, we first saw the Drass River. The weather was not clear, and we were yet to spot Tiger Hill.

First of all, we saw the place from where Bofor shells were fired during the Kargil War. The media also reported from this place often. I paid tribute to Captain Vikram Batra in my heart. Captain Vikram Batra of Jammu and Kashmir Rifles left an indelible mark in the Kargil War with his gallantry. For unprecedented bravery, he was awarded the

Param Vir Chakra. One of his interviews became very famous, in which he said, *"Yeh dil maange more."* That interview had taken place at this very place.

Even Pakistani soldiers trembled upon hearing his name and named him 'Shershah'. His anxiety and agony to free his land from Pakistan could clearly be seen in his eyes. He attained martyrdom while conquering peak 4875. Peak 4875 has been named 'Batra Top' after him.

After a short while, we entered Mushkoh Valley. It was this valley, which is famous for its unrivalled beauty, where Anuj Nayyar, a resident of Janakpuri, Delhi and captain of the Jat Regiment, sacrificed his life. But before dying a martyr's death, he had killed nine Pakistanis. He was posthumously awarded the Mahavir Chakra.

Major Vivek Gupta must be remembered as well. He made the supreme sacrifice while conquering Tololing. The next day, when his mortal remains were brought to Delhi, his wife, Dr Rajshree Gupta, who is also an army officer, arrived in uniform to salute him for the last time. For a wife to salute her husband's mortal remains in such an emotional moment reflected her commitment to duty, thinking, determination and courage. I salute Dr Rajshree's resolve and will never forget the photograph published in *India Today* during that time.

At the beginning of the war, the Indian Army suffered heavy losses. Thereafter, General V.P. Malik changed the strategy, and they started winning the lost posts one by one. When Lieutenant Vijayant Thapar of 2 Rajputana Rifles was sent to battle, he wrote a letter to his parents, saying that by the time they received his letter, the angels of heaven would be serving him. Perhaps he had an inkling that he would not return from the battlefield. And that is exactly what happened. He wrote two things in the letter that reflected his character: First, he had no regrets about dying. However, he wished that if he were born again, he would join the army again and serve the country. Secondly, he wanted people to visit Kargil and see how the soldiers sacrificed their today to secure their tomorrow. He was given the task of leading his men to capture the Three Pimples, Knoll and Lone Hill sections. Though they conquered Knoll, Vijayant Thapar lost his life to a burst of enemy fire. Vijayant Thapar belonged to a family of army officers. Both his father and grandfather served the country in the army. A main road in Noida has been named 'Shaheed Vijayant Thapar Marg' after him, who was a resident of Noida. Come what may, we must ensure that the martyrdom of our brave soldiers is never forgotten.

In this war, Sub Maj (Hon Capt) Yogendra Singh Yadav and Rifleman Sanjay Singh were also awarded the Param Vir Chakra for their undaunting bravery in the face of danger. Sub Maj (Hon Capt) Yogendra Singh, who received the Param Vir Chakra at the age of nineteen, is the youngest Param Vir Chakra awardee to date.

Our chairs and tables were placed at the foot of Tiger Hill for lunch. I was overwhelmed with the thought of how our soldiers could have climbed up the hill from there and overpowered the Pakistanis waiting in ambush above. They were at such a disadvantage, yet they remained undeterred. Indeed, only our passionately patriotic soldiers could realize victory in this war. They were praised by the Pentagon as well for their victory, which was truly extraordinary. After lunch, we visited the Drass War Memorial, where the belongings and weapons of the soldiers who fought in the war are on display.

Drass is the coldest place in India, where the temperature once went down to -60 degrees. I feel a shiver down my spine when I think about how our soldiers fought on those freezing nights during the war in sub-zero conditions. They had to be of another mettle. I bowed my head in reverence as I took in the landscape around me. Finally, we did see Tiger

Hill. Tiger Hill is a symbol of India's pride. It was very important for us to capture it because the Pakistanis could block National Highway 1 from there. If we had not captured it in time, the Leh and Siachen regions would have been in danger. The valiant soldiers of India once again rose to the occasion and defended the honour of the country and the tricolour with all their might.

After paying a heartfelt tribute to all the bravehearts at the war memorial, we started our return journey to Kargil. Major Sonam Wangchuk was another soldier who had emerged as a hero in this war. He led a successful operation against Pakistani troops in the Chorbat La pass on 31st May, which was the first successful operation of the war. Named the 'Lion of Ladakh', he was awarded the Mahavir Chakra for his heroic feat. I had the honour of meeting him personally during a programme of the Delhi Metro and NCC in 2008.

From the war memorial, Captain Singh showed us all those peaks which were much talked about during the Kargil War – Tololing, Batra Top, Sando Top, Rocky Knob, Three Pimples, Rhino Horn, 5140, India Gate, among others. By now, though we were physically tired, our spirits were still high because the day had turned out to be the most unforgettable day of our lives. Even after reaching the army guest house, I kept thinking about how brave our valiant soldiers were. To have been able to see the battleground for ourselves had been an overwhelming experience.

The next morning, we visited Complex 43. This complex is situated on the LOC, from where Pakistani soldiers can be clearly seen at their posts. While I was scanning the area there and taking pictures, some Pakistani soldiers came out of their posts and started looking at us. The soldiers on duty told us that before 1971, this area was with Pakistan, and whenever we wanted to send a truck to Leh, we had to get permission from Pakistan because the main and only road passed through this area.

However, after 1971, this process came to an end. 'There was a board on which was written 'POK' (Pakistan Occupied Kashmir) 600 metres'.

The weather was very clear and so we were able to see very far into the distance. From where we stood, we could clearly see the 11 Jhanda post of Pakistan in front. I was witnessing these sights for the first time in my life and had got the opportunity to see such an important border at such close quarters. That was indeed a memorable moment. Accumulating the memories, we returned to the mess.

Directly after lunch, we bid farewell to Kargil with a heavy heart and set out towards the final destination of our journey, i.e., Amarnath. After crossing Drass, we reached Zoji La Pass. Zoji La is the same place where during the Kashmir War of 1947, India had stunned the world when it used tanks with a strategy that was beyond the imagination of Pakistan. Today, when I remember Zoji La, my heart is filled with exhilaration.

In the 1999 war, 527 Indian soldiers made the supreme sacrifice, and 1,363 were injured. If one ever gets an opportunity, one must definitely visit these places and pay homage to the bravehearts. For their fortitude can never be forgotten. We only breathe in the air of freedom because of their valour. We must remain eternally grateful.

12

Indian Soldiers Honoured with the Param Vir Chakra

1. Major Somnath Sharma,* Indian Army Kumaon Regiment, 3rd November 1947, Budgam, Jammu and Kashmir
2. Naik Yadunath Singh,* Indian Army Rajput Regiment, 6th February 1948, Naushera, Jammu and Kashmir
3. Second Lieutenant Ram Raghoba Rane, Indian Army Corps of Engineers, 8th April 1948, Naushera, Jammu and Kashmir
4. Company Havildar Major Piru Singh Shekhawat,* Indian Army Rajputana Rifles, 17th July 1948, Tithwal, Jammu and Kashmir
5. Lance Naik Karam Singh, Indian Army, 13th October 1948, Tithwal, Jammu and Kashmir
6. Captain Gurbachan Singh Salaria,* Indian Army Gorkha Rifles, 5th December 1961, Elisabethville, Katanga, Congo
7. Major Dhan Singh Thapa, Indian Army Gorkha Rifles, 20th October 1962, Ladakh, Jammu and Kashmir, India
8. Subedar Joginder Singh,* Indian Army Sikh Regiment, 23rd October 1962, Tongpen La, NEFA, India
9. Major Shaitan Singh,* Indian Army Kumaon Regiment, 18th November 1962, Rezang La, Jammu and Kashmir
10. Master Quarter Company Havildar Abdul Hamid,* Indian Army The Grenadiers, 10th September 1965, Khemkaran Sector, India
11. Lieutenant Colonel Ardeshir Burzorji Tarapore, Indian Army Poona Horse, 11th September 1965, Phillaur Sector, Sialkot, Pakistan

12. Lance Naik Albert Ekka,* Indian Army Brigade of the Guards, 3rd December 1971, Ganga Sagar, West Bengal
13. Flying Officer Nirmal Jit Singh Sekhon,* Indian Air Force, 14th December 1971, Srinagar, Jammu and Kashmir
14. Second Lieutenant Arun Khetrapal,* Indian Army 17 Poona Horse, 16th December 1971, Bara Pind-Jarpal, Shakargarh Sector
15. Major Hoshiar Singh, Indian Army The Grenadiers, 17th December 1971, Basantar River, Shakargarh Sector
16. Naib Subedar Bana Singh, Indian Army Jammu and Kashmir Light Infantry, 23rd May 1987, Siachen Glacier, Jammu and Kashmir
17. Major Ramaswami Parmeshwaran,* Indian Army Mahar Regiment, 25th November 1987, Sri Lanka
18. Captain Manoj Kumar Pandey,* Indian Army Gorkha Rifles, 3rd July 1999, Khalubar/Juber Top Batalik Sector, Kargil, Jammu and Kashmir
19. Grenadier Yogendra Singh Yadav, Indian Army The Grenadiers, 4th July 1999, Tiger Hill, Kargil, Jammu and Kashmir
20. Rifleman Sanjay Kumar, Indian Army Jammu and Kashmir Rifles, 5th July 1999, Area Flat Top, Kargil, Jammu and Kashmir
21. Captain Vikram Batra,* Indian Army Jammu and Kashmir Rifles, 6th July 1999, Point 5140, Point 4875, Kargil, Jammu and Kashmir

*Posthumous

Important Sites of Revolution

The Revolution of 1857

- Barrackpore, West Bengal
- Jhansi, Uttar Pradesh
- Meerut, Uttar Pradesh
- Bithoor, Uttar Pradesh

- Kali Paltan Mandir, Meerut
- Pune, Maharashtra
- Yeola, Maharashtra
- Bhagur, Maharashtra
- Gwalior, Madhya Pradesh
- Kranti Tirth, Mandvi, Gujarat
- Vellore, Tamil Nadu
- Mutiny Memorial and Ajitgarh Memorial, New Delhi
- Red Fort, New Delhi

Hussainiwala, Ferozepur

- Shahidi Smarak, Hussainiwala Border, Ferozepur, Punjab
- Khatkar Kalan, Punjab
- Attari Border, Amritsar, Punjab
- Birthplace of Sukhdev Thapar, Chaura Bazar, Ludhiana, Punjab
- Kot Lakhpat, Rann of Kutch, Gujarat
- Leh, Jammu and Kashmir
- Museum, Rajguru Nagar, Maharashtra
- Chandra Shekhar Azad Nagar, Madhya Pradesh
- Chandrashekhar Park, Uttar Pradesh
- Netaji Bhawan, Kolkata, West Bengal

Kala Pani, Cellular Jail

- Cellular Jail, Andaman and Nicobar Islands
- Veer Savarkar Memorial, opposite Shivaji Park, Mumbai
- Birthplace of Veer Savarkar, Bhagur

Jalianwala Bagh and Attari Border

- Jallianwala Bagh, Punjab

- Golden Temple, Punjab
- Attari Border, Punjab
- Durgiana Mandir, Punjab

Indo-Pakistan War, 1947

- Zoji La Pass, Jammu and Kashmir
- Srinagar, Jammu and Kashmir
- Baltal, Jammu and Kashmir
- Kargil, Jammu and Kashmir
- Drass, Jammu and Kashmir
- Sonmarg, Jammu and Kashmir
- Naushera region, Jammu and Kashmir
- Budgam region, Jammu and Kashmir
- Tomb of Mohammad Osman (Jamia Milia Campus), New Delhi

Indo-China War of 1962

- Martyr Memorial, Chushul, Leh, Jammu and Kashmir
- Nathu La Pass, Sikkim
- Sela Pass, Arunachal Pradesh
- Bum La Pass, Tawang, Arunachal Pradesh
- Jaswant Singh Rawat War Memorial, Tawang, Arunachal Pradesh

Indo-Pakistan War of 1965

- Tomb of Veer Abdul Hamid, Asal Uttar, Punjab

Indo-Pakistan War of 1971

- Longewala and Tanot Mata Mandir, Rajasthan
- Diu, Daman and Diu
- Indian Air Force Museum and War Memorial, Palam, New Delhi

Kargil War of 1999

- Kargil Sector, Jammu and Kashmir
- Drass Sector, Jammu and Kashmir
- Batalik Sector, Jammu and Kashmir
- Srinagar, Jammu and Kashmir
- Siachen, Jammu and Kashmir
- Mushkoh Valley, Jammu and Kashmir
- Drass War Memorial, Drass, Jammu and Kashmir
- Zoji La Pass, Jammu and Kashmir
- Kala Pahar Outpost, Jammu and Kashmir
- Tiger Hill, Jammu and Kashmir
- Vijayant Thapar Memorial, Noida, Uttar Pradesh

List of War Memorials in India

PUNJAB

1. Vayu Shakti Sthal (Air Force Station), Adampur
2. Dograi War Memorial, Khasa Military Station, Amritsar
3. 5 Gorkha Rifles War Memorial, Amritsar
4. Pul Kanjari War Memorial, Amritsar
5. C Q M H. Abdul Hamid, P V C. Memorial, Asal Uttar
6. 7 Grenadiers War Memorial, Asal Uttar
7. Squadron Leader Ajay Ahuja Memorial, Air Force Station, Bhisiana, Bhatinda
8. 2 Lieutenant J.P. Gaur Memorial, Bhura Kuhna, Tarn Taran
9. 2 Madras Memorial, Bhura Kuhna, Tarn Taran
10. Sapper Harak Singh Memorial, Bhura Kuhna, Tarn Taran
11. Chandigarh War Memorial, Chandigarh
12. 1971 War Memorial, Asafwala, Fazilka

13. 1971 War Memorial, Sahjra, Ferozepur Cantonment
14. 1964 Memorial, Barki, Ferozepur
15. Saragarhi Memorial, Ferozepur
16. Sutlej Campaign War Memorial, Ferozepur
17. Mahar War Memorial, Mehandipur, Ferozepur
18. VI K.E.O. Cavalry War Memorial, Ferozepur
19. Brownlow's Punjabis War Memorial, Ferozepur
20. 19, 22 & 24 Punjabi War Memorial 1914-1999, Ferozepur
21. Squadron Leader Raman Uppal Memorial, Ferozepur
22. Gallipoli Memorial Tablet, Ferozepur
23. Batala War Memorial, Batala, Gurdaspur
24. 1971 War Memorial, Dera Baba Nanak, Gurdaspur
25. Halwara War Memorial, Halwara Air Force Station
26. National Martyrs Memorial, Hussainiwala
27. Lieutenant Jhaggar Singh War Memorial (WW-1), Kapurthala
28. Imperial State Forces War Memorial (WW-1), Kapurthala
29. Wall of Silence, Pathankot Air Force Station
30. Patiala State Forces Memorial, Patiala
31. Black Elephant Division Memorial, YPS Chowk, Patiala

JAMMU AND KASHMIR

1. Sikh War Memorial, Baramulla
2. Dagger Memorial, Baramulla
3. 8 Division Kargil War Memorial, Bimbat, Drass, Kargil
4. Condors War Memorial, Jammu
5. Balidan Stambh, Bahu Vali Rakh, Jammu
6. Tiger War Memorial, Jammu
7. War Memorial, Leh (1962, 1965, 1971 War)
8. War Memorial, Leh (1947-48)

9. Sahi Memorial Hospital, Machail
10. Lok Bahadur Stadium Memorial, Poonchh
11. Hall-of-Fame, Rajauri
12. 3 Madras Memorial, Samba
13. 2/Lieutenant Arun Khetarpal, PVC War Memorial, Samba
14. Major R.S. Rajawat Memorial, Samba
15. Jammu and Kashmir State Forces War Memorial, Satwari Cantonment
16. Siachen War Memorial, Siachen Base Camp, Ladakh
17. Rezang La War Memorial, Rezang La, Ladakh
18. Srinagar War Memorial, Srinagar Air Force Station
19. 15 Corps War Memorial, Srinagar
20. Dhruva Shaheed Smarak, Udhampur
21. Operation Rakshak Memorial, BB Cantonment, Srinagar
22. Chushul War Memorial, Chushul, Ladakh

Uttar Pradesh

1. Shatrujit War Memorial (Para Brigade), Agra
2. 4 Infantry Division War Memorial (Hall of Fame in Old Cantonment), Allahabad
3. Indian Airforce Central Air Command War Memorial, Allahabad
4. Jat Regiment War Memorial, Bareilly
5. C.M.P. x 7 Infantry Brigade War Memorial, Faizabad
6. Dogra War Memorial, Faizabad
7. Headquarters 7 Infantry Brigade War Memorial, Faizabad
8. Sikh Light Infantry War Memorial, Farrukhabad
9. Rajput Regiment War Memorial, Fatehgarh
10. Airforce Station War Memorial, Gorakhpur
11. White Tiger War Memorial, Jhansi Cant

12. Gorkha Brigade War Memorial, Kunraghat, Gorakhpur
13. Armed Forces Medical Services War Memorial, Lucknow
14. Smritika War Memorial, Lucknow
15. 11 Gorkha Rifles War Memorial, Lucknow
16. 1 Corps War Memorial, Mathura
17. Pine Division War Memorial, Meerut Cantonment
18. Saragarhi Memorial, Meerut Cantonment
19. Noida Shaheed Smarak, Noida
20. Air Force Station Sarsawa War Memorial, Sarsawa, Saharanpur
21. 39 Gorkha Training Centre War Memorial, Varanasi

Rajasthan

1. Alwar War Memorial, Alwar
2. Shaheed Smarak Memorial, Churu
3. Sadhewala War Memorial, Jaipur
4. Shaheed Smarak War Memorial, Jaipur
5. Amar Jawan Jyoti War Memorial, Jaipur
6. Vijay Stambh, Vijay Smarak, Jaisalmer
7. Konark War Memorial, Jodhpur
8. Major Shaitan Singh PVC. Memorial, Jodhpur
9. Longewala War Memorial, Longewala
10. War Memorial B.P. 638, Longewala Sector
11. 168 F.D. Regiment War Memorial, Longewala
12. Nagi War Memorial, Shri Ganganagar

New Delhi

1. National War Memorial, India Gate
2. Teen Murti Haifa Memorial, Teen Murti Road
3. India Gate

4. Rajputana Rifles War Memorial, Rajputana Rifles Regimental Centre
5. Air Force Station, Palam War Memorial, Near Air Force Museum, Palam

Karnataka

1. Madras Sappers War Memorial, Bangalore
2. Army Service Corps War Memorial, Bangalore
3. Army Transport Animals Memorial, Bangalore
4. Corps of Military Police War Memorial, Bangalore
5. Pioneer Corps War Memorial, Bangalore
6. Indian Air Force Training Command Memorial, Bangalore
7. British War Memorial, Bangalore
8. Parachute Regiment War Memorial, Bangalore
9. Maratha Light Infantry War Memorial, Belgam
10. Air Force Station Bidar Memorial, Bidar
11. Karwar Anjediva Island War Memorial, Anjediva Island

Gujarat

1. Golden Katar War Memorial, Ahmedabad Cantonment
2. Ahmedabad War Memorial, Ahmedabad
3. Bhuj War Memorial, Bhuj
4. Parbat Ali War Memorial, Gandhinagar
5. Vijay Stambh, Jamnagar
6. I.N.S. Valsura War Memorial, Jamnagar
7. Air Force Station Jamnagar War Memorial, Jamnagar

Madhya Pradesh

1. No. 3 E.M.E. Centre War Memorial, Bhopal
2. Sudarshan Chakra War Memorial, Bhopal

3. Corps of Signal War Memorial, Jabalpur
4. The Grenadiers War Memorial, Jabalpur
5. Jammu and Kashmir Rifles War Memorial, Jabalpur
6. Kanglatongbi War Memorial, Jabalpur
7. Infantry Memorial, Mahu
8. Shahbaz War Memorial, Saugor

Maharashtra

1. Armed Corps War Memorial, Ahmednagar
2. Mechanised Infantry Regiment War Memorial, Ahmednagar
3. The Mahar Regiment War Memorial, Kamptee
4. Hut of Remembrance, Khadakwasla, Pune
5. Bombay Pioneer Memorial (WW-1), Kirkee
6. Bombay Sappers War Memorial, Kirkee
7. I.N.S. Shivaji War Memorial, Lonavala, Pune
8. Naval Uprising Memorial, 30 Woodehouse Road, Mumbai
9. Subedar Joginder Singh P.V.C. Memorial, Military Station Colaba
10. Artillery Centre War Memorial, Nasik Road Camp
11. Morwada War Memorial, Pune Cantonment
12. 45 C.A.V. Memorial, Southern Command A.O.R.

Haryana

1. Air Force Station Ambala, Ambala
2. Veer Smriti Western Command War Memorial, Chandi Mandir Cant.
3. Gurgaon Shaheed Sthal, Gurgaon
4. Amar Jawan War Memorial, Hissar
5. Jhajjar War Memorial, Jhajjar
6. Jind War Memorial, Jind
7. Narwana War Memorial, Narwana

8. Rezang La War Memorial, Gurugram
9. Bahadurgarh War Memorial, Bahadurgarh
10. Yuddha Shaheed Smarak, Rohtak

Arunachal Pradesh

1. Helmet Top War Memorial, 18 Km from Walong
2. Manmao War Memorial, Manmao Post
3. Jaswant Garh War Memorial, Nura Nang
4. Tawang War Memorial, Tawang
5. Walong War Memorial, Walong
6. Hut of Remembrance, Walong
7. Air Force Memorial Walong, Walong

Jharkhand

1. Saragarhi War Memorial, Ramgarh Cantonment
2. Sikh Regiment War Memorial, Ramgarh Cantonment
3. Punjab Regiment War Memorial, Ramgarh Cantonment
4. Jharkhand War Memorial, Ranchi

Andhra Pradesh

1. Air Force Academy Flight Crew Memorial, Dundigal, Hyderabad
2. Basantar War Memorial, Hyderabad
3. 1 E.M.E. Centre War Memorial, Secunderabad Cantonment
4. A.O.C. Centre War Memorial, Secunderabad
5. Veerula Sainik Smarak, Secunderabad
6. Mighty Bombardiers War Memorial, Secunderabad
7. Victory At Sea War Memorial, Vishakhapatnam

Meghalaya

1. 58 Gorkha Training Centre War Memorial, Shillong
2. Assam Regiment War Memorial, Shillong

3. 1971 War Memorial, Shillong

West Bengal

1. Bogra War Memorial, Binnaguri
2. Batasia Loop War Memorial, Darjeeling
3. Air Force Station Hasimara War Memorial, Hasimara, Jalpaiguri
4. Lascar War Memorial, Howrah
5. The Glorious Dead War Memorial, Kolkata
6. 49 Bengali War Memorial, Kolkata
7. Eastern Command Vijay Smarak, Kolkata
8. 33 Corps Vijay Smarak War Memorial, Sukna Military Station

Uttarakhand

1. Indian Military Academy War Memorial, Dehradun
2. Lal Gate War Memorial, Dehradun
3. Garhwal Rifles War Memorial, Lansdowne
4. Maharaj K Memorial Park, Pithoragarh
5. Kumaon Regiment War Memorial, Ranikhet
6. Bengal Sappers War Memorial, Roorkee

Himachal Pradesh

1. Dharmshala Shaheed Smarak, Dharmshala
2. 3 Mountain Artillery Brigade War Memorial (WW-1), Shimla
3. 14 G.T.C. War Memorial, Subathu

Assam

1. D.A.H. War Memorial, Dibrugarh
2. Air Force Station Guwahati War Memorial, Guwahati
3. Air Force Station Mohanbari War Memorial, Mohanbari
4. Amar Jawan War Memorial, Silchar
5. Air Force Station Tezpur War Memorial, Tezpur

6. 4 Corps War Memorial, Tezpur

Tamil Nadu

1. Air Force Station Awadi Kargil War Memorial, Avadi, Chennai
2. WW-1 War Memorial, Tiruchirappalli
3. Madras Regiment War Memorial, Wellington

Kerala

1. Defence Security Corps Gaurav Sthal, Kannur
2. Indian Naval Academy Ezhimala War Memorial, Ezhimala
3. I.N.S. Venduruthy War Memorial, Kochi
4. The Bogra Memorial Hut, Thiruvananthapuram

Tripura

1. Agartala War Memorial, Agartala

Bihar

1. Bihar Regiment War Memorial, Danapur, Bihar

Diu

1. I.N.S. Khukri Memorial

Manipur

1. Kangla Tongbi War Memorial, Khengjang, Imphal
2. Shanti Van War Memorial, Leimakhong

Nagaland

1. Orchid Memorial, Zakhama Military Station

*Source: List made available on the internet by the Ministry of External Affairs, Government of India

References

- *Guns and Glory Series: India's Wars*. Headlines Today.
- *Pradhanmantri Series*. ABP NEWS (presented by Shekhar Kapoor)
- *Chander Shekhar Azad*. Documentary by Ministry of Information & Broadcasting
- *History of Cellular Jail – Kālā Pānī*. Documentary by Ministry of Information & Broadcasting.
- *Shahid Bhagat Singh – The Story of the Legend*. Documentary by Live Himmatpura.
- *Shaheed Bhagat Singh*. Documentary by Navalpreet Rangi.
- *Madan Lal Dhingra*. Documentary by Darshan Lal Jain.
- *A Tribute to Shaheed Bhagat Singh – The Ever-Loved National Hero*. Documentary by Ministry of Information & Broadcasting.
- *PM Modi visits National Martyrs Memorial at Hussainiwala village in Ferozepur, Punjab*. Narendra Modi Channel.
- *Param Vir Chakra*. A serial produced by Chetan Anand for Doordarshan.
- Films made on the life of Bhagat Singh.

Information was obtained from following museums/monuments:

- Indian Air Force Museum, Palam Road, Near Hanuman Mandir, Palam, New Delhi
- National Archives Museum, Janpath Road, New Delhi
- Nehru Memorial Museum, Teen Murti Bhawan, New Delhi

- Indira Gandhi Memorial Museum, 1 Safdarjung Road, New Delhi
- Mutiny Memorial, near Hindu Rao Hospital and Badli ki Sarai, near Adarsh Nagar Metro
- Nicholson Cemetery, Club Road, Civil Lines, New Delhi
- Information gathered from Bhagat Singh, Rajguru and Veer Savarkar Museum
- Government Freedom Struggle Museum, Meerut, Uttar Pradesh
- Freedom Struggle Museum, Red Fort, Delhi
- Freedom Fighter's Museum, Red Fort, Delhi
- Indian War Memorial Museum, Red Fort, Delhi
- Mumtaz Mahal Museum
- Mutiny Memorial, Kashmiri Gate, Delhi
- Birthplace and Museum of Chandra Shekhar Azad, Chandra Shekhar Azad Nagar, Madhya Pradesh

Books:

- Mande, Lt General Yashwant. *Shreshtha Sainik Kahaniyan*, Prabhat Prakashan, New Delhi.
- Anil Kumar, ed. *Mein Bhagat Singh Bol Raha Hun*, Pratibha Pratishthan, New Delhi.
- Verma Shiv. *Sansmrutiya*, National Book Trust of India.
- Saxena Balbir. *Param Veer Vijeta*, Mansi Prakashan, New Delhi.
- Sood, Major General Shubhi. *Bhartiya Sena ke Shurveer*, Prabhat Prakashan, New Delhi.
- Kumar, Dinkar. *Mahakrantikari Mangal Pandey*, Children Book Temple, Delhi.
- Patoriya, Rajendra. *Netaji Subhash: Chitramay Jeevani*, Vidya Vihar, New Delhi.

- Sharma, Mahesh. *Amar Balidani Tatya Tope*, Prabhat Paperbacks, New Delhi.
- Sanyal, Jitendranath. *Amar Shahid Sardar Bhagat Singh*, National Book Trust of India.
- Murli Manohar Prasad Singh, Rekha Awasthi, ed. *1857: Itihas aur Sanskriti*, Publications Division, Ministry of Information and Broadcasting, Government of India.
- Sen, Surendranath. *Atharah Sau Sattavan ka Swatantrya Sangram*, Publications Division, Ministry of Information and Broadcasting, Government of India.
- Singh, Jaswant and Major General Suraj Bhatia, *Shauryam Tejo*, Prabhat Prakashan, Delhi.
- Sahni, Bhishm. *Rang De Basanti Chola*, Pustakghar Prakashan, New Delhi.
- Damodar Savarkar, Vinayak *Kālā Pānī*, Prabhat Prakashan, New Delhi.
- Singh, General J.J. *Ek Sena Adhyaksh ki Atmkatha*, Prabhat Prakashan, New Delhi.
- Verma, Shiv Kunal. *1962: The War That Wasn't* (e-book), Aleph Book Company.
- Waraich, Malwinder Jit Singh and Harish Jain. *Bhagat Singh's 'Jail Note Book'*, Unistar Books Pvt. Ltd.
- Waraich, Malwinder Jit Singh. *Bhagat Singh: The Eternal Rebel*, Unistar Books Pvt. Ltd.
- Maclean, Kama. *A Revolutionary History of Interwar India*, Penguin Books.